A DICTIONARY

OF THE PROPER NAMES OF THE OLD AND
NEW TESTAMENT SCRIPTURES, BEING
AN ACCURATE AND LITERAL
TRANSLATION FROM THE
ORIGINAL TONGUES

By

J. B. JACKSON

LOIZEAUX BROTHERS
Neptune, New Jersey

THIRD EDITION, SEPTEMBER 1957
NINTH PRINTING, NOVEMBER 1987

ISBN 0-87213-410-5
PRINTED IN THE UNITED STATES OF AMERICA

20   19   18   17   16   15   14   13   12   11

PREFACE

Some years since, the present writer, in pursuing his studies in the Bible, reached a portion which consisted largely of Proper Names, and at once he was confronted with the fact, that a considerable and, to him, important portion of the Bible was untranslated.

Fully persuaded that "whatsoever things were written aforetime were written for our learning," and that "all Scripture is given by inspiration of God, and is profitable for doctrine" (Rom. 15: 4 — 2 Tim. 3: 16); and hence that there could be no idle word in God's Book; he set about preparing an accurate, alphabetical list of all the Proper Names of the Old and New Testaments, with a view to securing the best possible renderings of the same.

Fortunately, there was ready access to the works of Cruden, Long, Oliver, Young, Wilkinson, Charnock, McClintock & Strong, Smith's Bible Dictionary, Abbott's Dictionary, Imperial Bible Dictionary, Encyclopedia Biblica, and, before the list was complete, Strong's Concordance, Tregelles, F. W. Grant, and others.

At the end of about three years, the writer had obtained a meaning for nearly every proper name in the Bible, and, on the recommendation of friends, began preparations for publishing the results of his labors, for the benefit of others similarly interested.

His plan was to arrange the names alphabetically, as spelled in our common English Bibles, attaching the meanings he had found, in the order in which he considered them to have weight, *i.e.*, in the order in which he considered their sources to be authoritative.

At the end of this part of his work, ere he went to press with his new Onomasticon, it occurred to him to experiment a little with some of the meanings he had secured, in order to see how they would work in the elucidation of some of those passages which had first suggested the need of his researches.

The result was as perplexing as it was curious; in some cases no less than twelve different, not to say *opposite*, meanings were given to the same name, *by the same writer*. But which, if any one of them, was the English equivalent of the Hebrew or Greek name under consideration?

That was the important question, to determine which, a few of these names were subjected to rigid, etymological analysis; during which, two discoveries were made, viz.:

1. That not one of these Onomasticographers could be depended upon throughout his whole list of names.

2. That "every Scripture was God-inspired . . . that the man of God may be perfect, fully fitted to every good work." (2 Tim. 3: 16, 17 — literal rendering.)

A new start was made; *all* meanings were discarded, and each name was traced to its own roots in the original tongue, and the meaning derived according to the etymological rules and usage of the language in which it was written.

In the present work all current authorities have been used or consulted, such as Robinson's Gesenius, Fuerst's Hebrew Lexicon, Davidson's Hebrew and Chaldee Lexicon, Davies' Hebrew Lexicon, and now that it is completed, the learned and laborious Hebrew and Chaldee Lexicon, by Brown, Driver & Briggs; as well as Tregelles and some others for portions.

For the New Testament names, the Greek Lexicons of Liddell & Scott, and Parkhurst, have been mainly relied upon.

The one controlling idea in the preparation of this work has been to provide the English-speaking reader with an exact, literal equivalent of the original Hebrew, Chaldee (Aramaic), or Greek name; and this the reader may expect to find.

In each and every case the author has compared his rendering with the rendering given by the Onomasticographers above mentioned, and where he differs from them he is quite prepared to give a satisfactory reason for the difference, to any one competent to form a judgment.

Where such different rendering is possible or plausible, he has not failed to give it a place with his own.

In addition to this, he has carefully noted each meaning as related to its context, since the passage in which a name occurs will often throw light upon the particular shade of meaning to be given to it.

As an illustration of how the present writer finds it necessary to differ from men of unquestioned scholarship, the name "Abijam" may be instanced: —

One of the ablest of modern Hebraists, in his Manual of Hebrew, gives the meaning "great sailor," from *a b i*, meaning "father of" (being *ab* in the construct state, and *ab* means "father"), and *y a m*, meaning "sea," *i.e.*, "father of the sea."

Now the scholarship of the author of the Manual is above question, as a Hebraist he had few equals, and he knew perfectly well that the *literal* force of those two words was "father of the sea," and that they would, etymologically, admit of no other meaning whatever (if we allow the single exception of "my father *is* the sea," there is nothing in the words themselves to exclude such a meaning), but at once the learned professor allows himself to be swayed by the apparent strangeness of the name, and tapers it down to "great sailor," losing sight of the original words entirely.

Of what use is the most eminent scholarship, if, with all its ability to give us bread, it give us but a stone?

By far the best work on Proper Names known to the writer is that by Mr. Alfred Jones, published by Bagster & Sons.

It treats only the names in the Old Testament, and not a few of those are omitted, for some reason, but the plan, as well as the typographical execution of the work, are excellent, although the result is frequently disappointing, and in more ways than one, particularly in the author's arriving at the proper literal meaning, by his analysis, and then, for reasons other than etymological, leaving a meaning for the name which loses sight of the origin entirely, as for example: —

"'Omar' = 'uppermost,' from the Hithpæl of the

root *a m a r;* it is generally understood of 'he that speaks,' hence Gesenius says, 'eloquent,' 'talkative.'"

Now the verb *a m a r* is a very common one, and is invariably rendered "to say, to utter"; in the Hithpael it is twice used in the sense of 'boasting self,' as in Ps. 94: 4, but to call Omar a Hithpael is a mere blunder; it is an orthographic variation of Kal participle active, and means "saying," or "sayer," but not a trace of this meaning in "uppermost." Another example from this otherwise excellent work may suffice: —

"'Bealoth' = 'city corporations,' *i.e.*, 'rulers,' 'civitates,' or perhaps 'daughters of the city,' plural of *b a a l a h* = 'mistress' fem of *B a a l* — 'lord,' 'possessor,'" *i.e.*, the plural of 'mistress' is 'city corporations'(!).

Here again the plain, literal meaning (and a meaning which the learned author himself sees plainly enough) is discarded, and we are left with "city corporations," although there is not a trace of either 'city' or 'corporations' in the word discussed. And this so often: and yet it is not his scholarship which is at fault, scholarship is rarely, if ever, at fault in the rendering of Proper Names in the Bible, but rather what this excellent author says himself very fittingly, quoting from Mr. Bryant, under the article "Chaldeans": —

"So far does whim get the better of judgment (in deriving the meanings of proper names), that even the written word is not safe."

In the present work, the meanings are, in general, given in the language of the Authorized Version, but occasionally, where the Authorized Version fails to convey the leading thought of the root, another more suitable word has been chosen.

Smoothness of expression has not been sought, nor a learned treatise, but simply and solely to put the English reader in possession of the exact sense of the original: for this reason many of the meanings may sound harsh, from their very bald literality.

It may be remarked that some Hebrew roots are susceptible of two or even more entirely different meanings, as *e.g.*, *a n a h*, a word very frequently used, in many places translated "answer," "respond," but as commonly rendered "afflict"; in such cases the alternative rendering has been given.

Again, some names are capable of being derived, with equal accuracy, from two, or even three different roots, as *e.g.*, when the root is one with a feeble radical, or doubles the second radical, the inflection of such verbs being to some extent similar: but where an alternative rendering has been thought possible, it has been given.

Furthermore, as a large proportion of both Hebrew and Greek Proper Names are compounds, it may be necessary to remark that these compounds are capable of being put together differently, as *e.g.*, Caleb, which may be an orthographic variation of *caleb* = "dog," or it may, with equal propriety, be derived from *c o l* = "all," and *l e b* = "heart," whence "all-heart" (whole-hearted), but such cases are all noted.

In a much larger work now in preparation, the analysis of each word is given in full, and the etymological processes by which each meaning is arrived at, with every occurrence of each name (when not exceeding twelve), and historical, geographical and other references, where such are found, or appear useful, in addition to some illustrations of how Proper Names are helpful, and indeed essential, in the elucidation of the sacred text: to this the interested Bible student is referred, particularly such as are more or less acquainted with the original languages, and desire to satisfy themselves as to the correctness of the renderings.

Spiritual judgment, as well as scholarship, is absolutely essential in translating the Word of God from one tongue into another, and the writer claims no monopoly of either, but will welcome friendly criticism from any who are sufficiently interested and competent to form a judgment.

To such as are likely to use this little work, little need be said as to the importance of an exact, literal translation of the Proper Names of the Bible: without such translation, many chapters in our Bibles remain but a morass of unintelligible jargon, difficult to pronounce, as *e.g.*, Josh. 19 and 1 Chron. 1 and 2, etc., whereas, if we are to believe 2 Tim. 3: 16, there is *teaching* in all this, and besides, we are again and again shown the importance attaching to the meaning of a name, as *e.g.*: —

1. on its *imposition*, as in the case of Isaac (Gen. 17: 19, cf. v. 17), and of Jesus (Matt. 1: 21);

2. on its being *changed*, as in Abram (Gen. 17: 5), see also the change of Jacob's name (Gen. 32: 28);

3. on the *play* upon a name, as in Jer. 1: 11, 12, where the play is rather upon a word, obscured in

our English Bible, but it is really, "I see a rod of a *s h a q e d* tree," "I am *s h a q e d* my word to perform it," *i.e.,* "I see a rod of a *waking* tree, — I am *waking* my word to perform it."

Ezek. 23: 4, affords an example of play upon names. Had we been left to the Old Testament history alone, we might have thought Melchizedek too obscure and isolated to require any further study than the immediate context of Gen. 14: 18, 19: the meaning of his name, and that of his kingdom being of no importance whatever; but the Spirit of God has seen fit to enlarge upon both the meaning of his name and that of his kingdom, as well as the *order* in which the names occur.

The fact that Elijah (my God is Jah) is followed by Elisha (my God is salvation), the connection between the two prophets, and the different dealing of the Lord under each, would be but very imperfectly understood apart from the significance of their names.

Trusting that the reader of this work may, by its means, gather some of the precious fruits it has been the writer's privilege to enjoy in its preparation, it is now sent forth commended to the care of Him whose grace has ever been found sufficient through the eleven years spent upon it.

If it shall, through grace, be the means of removing, in any little measure, the veil which our confused speech has put upon His precious word, the labor will not have been in vain, and to Him be all the praise.

THE AUTHOR.

BOSTON, *March*, 1908.

PRONUNCIATION

1. Sound a as *a* in " father "
   e " *a* " " fate "
   i " *ee* " " feet "
   (short) o " *o* " " lot "
   (long) o " *o* " " bone "
   u " *oo* " " cool "
   ch " *k* (save in the words " cherub," " cherubim "
and " Rachel," which from long usage have become Anglicized:
here *ch* is sounded like *ch* in cheer; but "Cherub," a city, is
pronounced " Ke′rub.")

Examples:

          Baruch, pronounced " Bah′ rook "
          Ches′ a lon, as " Kes′ a lon "

2. In Hebrew proper names, G is hard before *e*, *i* and *y*, as
" Gideon," " Gibeah "; except " Bethpage," which, having
passed through the Greek tongue of the N. T. is subject to the
rule applying to words from the Greek, whence " Beth phage "
(as in " cage ").

3. The diphthong *ei* is pronounced like *ee* " Keilah " (Kee′lah).
When *ei* is followed by a vowel, the *i* is usually sounded like
y consonant: as Iphideiah (If e de′ yah); the termination *iah*, in
O. T. names, nearly always taking that sound, from the coales-
cing of the two sounds " ee " and " ah " = " yah."

4. The consonants *c*, *s*, and *t*, before *ia* and *iu*, preceded by
the accent, in most Scripture names, take the sound of " sh "
(zh): as Cappadocia (sha), Galatia (sha), Asia (zha), Tertius
(shus).

DICTIONARY OF PROPER NAMES

Aa'ron, light-bringer
Aa'ron ites, patronymic of preceding
A bad'don, destruction
A bag'tha, father of the wine-press
A ba'na, constancy: a sure ordinance
Ab'arim, regions beyond: the passages
Ab'ba, father
Ab'da, service
Ab'de el, servant of God
Ab'di, my servant
Ab'di el, servant of God
Ab'don, servitude
A bed'ne go, servant of brightness
A'bel (2d son of Adam), vanity (*i.e.*, transitory)
A'bel (2), mourning, or a meadow
A'bel beth ma'a chah, mourning (or " meadow ") of the house of oppression
A'bel ker a'mim, mourning of the vineyards
A'bel ma'im, mourning of the waters
A'bel me ho'lah, mourning of dancing
A'bel miz ra'im, mourning of the Egyptians
A'bel shit'tim, mourning of the acacias
A'bez, I will make white (or miry)
A'bi, my father (or fatherly)
A bi'a, my father is Jah
A bi'ah, same as preceding
A'bi al'bon, my father is above understanding or " father of understanding "
A bi'a saph, father of the gatherer
A bi'a thar, father of abundance, or " father of a remnant "
A'bib, green ear (of corn)

1

A bi′da, father of knowledge
A bi′dah, father of knowledge
A bi′dan, father of the judge
A bi′el, my father is God
A′bi e′zer, father of help
A′bi ez′rite, patronymic of preceding
Ab′i gail, father of joy
Ab′i gail (2), father of a heap (or " billow ") in 2 Sam. 17: 25
A bi ha′il, father of howling (or " of shining forth "), probably
        textual error for following
A bi ha′il (2) father of valor (endurance)
A bi′hu, my father is he, or " father of *him* "
A bi′hud, father of majesty
A bi′jah, my father is Jah
A bi′jam, father of the sea
A bi le′ne, without books, or without king
A bim′a el, my father is what god? or my father is from God
A bim′e lech, my father is king
A bin′a dab, father of the willing giver
Ab′i ner, my father is a lamp
A bin′o am, father of pleasantness
A bi′ram, my father is exalted
A bi′shag, my father erred
A bi′shai, father of gift
A bi sha′lom, father of peace
A bi shu′a, father of salvation, or of riches
A bi′shur, father of beholding, or father of the singer
A bi′tal, father of dew
Ab′i tub, father of goodness
A bi′ud, Greek form of Abihud
Ab′ner, father of a lamp (1 Sam. 14: 50)
Ab′ner (2), father is a lamp
A′bra ham, father of a great multitude
Ab′ram, father is exalted
Ab′rech, I will cause blessing, or tender father
Ab′sa lom, father is peace
Ac′cad, only a pitcher
Ac′cho, his straitness

A cel′da ma, field of blood
A cha′ia, wailing
A cha′i cus, derivative of preceding
A′chan, thought to mean same as Achar
A′char, troubler
A′chaz, Greek form of Ahaz
Ach′bor, a mouse
A′chim, without winter
A′chish, I will blacken (or terrify), or " only a man "
Ach′me tha, brother of death
A′chor, to trouble
Ach′sa }
Ach′sah, } to tinkle, or anklet
Ach′shaph, I shall be bewitched
Ach′zib, I shall make a lie
A da′dah, forever adorned, or the prey adorned
A′dah, ornament, or he adorned
A da i′ah, adorned of Jah
Ad al i′ah, I shall be drawn up of Jah
A′dam, man: red earth
A da′mah, the earth, ground
A da′mi, man of (add following word)
A′dar, glorious
A′dar (2), exceeding glorious (Josh. 15: 3 only)
Ad′be el, chastened of God
Ad′dan, their hap
Ad′dar, same as Adar 2
Ad′di, Greek for Adah
Ad′don, misfortune
A′der, musterer, care-taker; a flock
A′di el, ornament of God
A′din, given to pleasure
A di′na, voluptuous
A di′no, his ornament, his luxuriousness
A di tha′im, double ornament
Ad′lai, the prey is mine
Ad′mah, earthiness
Ad′ma tha, her earthiness: man's chamber (?)

Ad′na, pleasure
Ad′nah, pleasure
Ad′nah, (2) resting forever (1 Ch. 12: 20 only)
A do ni be′zek, lord of lightning
A do ni′jah, my lord is Jah (Jehovah)
A do ni′kam, lord of rising up; my lord has arisen
A do ni′ram, my lord is high
A do ni ze′dec, lord of righteousness
A do ra′im, double glory
A do′ram, their glory
A dram′me lech, the glorious king: glory of the king
Ad′ra myt′ti um, not in the race: I shall abide in death
A′dri a, without wood
A′dri el, flock of God: my shepherder is God
A dul′lam, a testimony to them
A dul′lam ite, patronymic of preceding
A dum′mim, ruddy ones: quieted ones (?)
Ae′neas, to praise
Ae′non, to praise, but if from Hebrew " fountain "
Ag′ab us, a grasshopper
A′gag, I will overtop
A′gag ite, gentilic of preceding
A′gar, Greek form of Hagar
A′gee, I shall increase
A grip′pa, horse-hunter
A′gur, gathered
A′hab, brother of father
A har′ah, brother of breathing: remaining brother
A har′hel, behind the wall
A ha′sai, my possessions
A has′bai, brother of my encompassers: I will take refuge in my (arms)
A has u e′rus, I will be silent and poor
A ha′va, I shall subsist
A′haz, possessor
A′haz i′ ah, possessed of Jehovah
Ah′ban, brother of understanding
A′her, another

A'hi, my brother
A hi'ah, brother of Jehovah,
A hi'am, brother of mother
A hi'an, brother of them
A hi e'zer, brother of help
A hi'hud, brother of majesty
A hi' hud (2), brother of the propounder (of riddles): my brother is united (1 Ch. 8:7)
A hi'jah, brother of Jehovah
A hi'kam, brother of rising
A hi'lud, brother of travail: brother of one born
A him'a az, brother of counsel
A hi'man, brother of a portion: brother of whom?
A him'e lech, brother of the king
A hi'moth, brother of death
A hi'na dab, brother of the willing giver
A hin'o am, brother of pleasantness
A hi'o, brotherly (literally brother of *him*)
A hi'ra, brother of evil
A hi'ram, brother of lifting up
A hi'ram ite, patronymic of preceding
A his'am ach, brother of support
A hi'sha har, brother of the morning
A hi'shar, brother of the singer
A hi'tho phel, brother of folly
A hi'tub, brother of goodness
Ah'lab, I shall be made fat
Ah'lai, O, would that
A ho'ah, brother of rest (?)
A hoh'ite, patronymic of preceding
A ho'lah, her own tent
A ho'li ab, tent of father
A hol'i bah, my tent is in her
A ho li ba'mah, tent of the high place
A hu'mai, a water reed: brother of waters
A hu'zam, their possession
A huz'zath, possession
A'i, the heap (of ruins)

A i'ah, falcon: kite
A i'ath, a heap
A i'ja, heap of ruins
A i'ja lon, deer-field: a large stag
A i'je leth sha'har, the hind of the morning
A'in, an eye: fountain
Ai'tam, ravenous beast consumed (?) (a name in LXX of Josh.
    xv. 60)
A'jah, same as Aiah
Aj'a lon, same as Aijalon
A'kan, oppression
Ak'kub, subtle (literally to take by the heel)
Ak rab'bim, scorpions
Al'am eth, concealment
A lam'melech, the king's oak
Al'am oth, virgins (as *covered*): hiding places
A le'meth, same as Alameth
Al ex an'der, man-defender
Al ex an'dri a, derivative of preceding
Al ex an'dri ans, gentilic of preceding.
Al'gum, not added ones (?): not drunken ones
A li'ah, above is Jah: iniquity
Al'i an, my surpassing them (?): or i.q. Alvan
Al le lu'ia, Greek for praise ye Jah
Al'lon, an oak
Al'lon Bach'uth, oak of weeping
Al mo'dad, not measured
Al'mon, concealment
Al'mon Dib lath a'im, concealment of the two fig cakes
Al'mug, not dissolved
A'loth, the heights: mistresses
Al'pha, first letter of the Greek alphabet: beginning
Al phe'us, produce: gain: if from Hebrew = my exchanges
Al tas'chith, thou mayest not destroy
A'lush, I will knead (bread)
Al'vah, iniquity: above is Jah
Al'van, their ascent: iniquitous one
A'mad, people of eternity

A'mal, perverseness

Am'al ek, people of lapping (or licking up)

Am al'ek ites, gentilic of preceding

A'mam, their mother

A ma'na, constancy: a settled provision

Am a ri'ah, the saying of Jehovah

A ma'sa, burdensome (?)

A mas'a i, my burdens

A mash'a i, people of my spoilers

A mas.i'ah, laden of Jah

A maz i'ah, strength of Jah

A'men, truth

Am'e thyst, dream-stone (literally I shall be brought back — as from a dream)

A'mi, bond-servant

A min'a dab, Greek form of Amminadab

A mit'tai, my faithfulness

Am'mah, a cubit

Am'mi, my people

Am mi'el, my people are of God

Am mi'hud, people of majesty

Am mi'hud (2), my people is white (in 2 Sam. 13: 37 where some copies have preceding)

Am min'a dab, people of the willing-giver

Am min'a dib, my people are willing

Am mi shad'da i, people of the Almighty

Am miz'a bad, people of the endower

Am'mon, tribal (*peoplish*)

Am'mon ite-s, gentilic of preceding

Am'mo ni tess, feminine of preceding

Am'non, faithful

Am'non (2), made faithful (in 2 Sam. 13: 20)

A'mok, to be deep

A'mon, to nourish: to be faithful

Am'or ite, a sayer

A'mos, to lade, to burden

A'moz, to be strong, courageous

Am phip'o lis, around the city

Am'pli as, enlarged
Am'ram, the people is exalted
Am'ram (2), their slime: their heaping up (1 Ch. 1: 41)
Am'ram ite, patronymic of Amram (1)
Am'ra phel, sayer of darkness: fall of the sayer
Am'zi, my strength
A'nab, grape-ish (grape-dom)
A'nah, afflicted: answered
An a ha'rath, the groaning of fear
An a i'ah, afflicted (or answered) of Jah
A'nak, neck-chain: long-necked
An'a kim, patronymic of preceding
An'am im, affliction (or answer) of the waters
A nam'me lech, the affliction of the king
A'nan, a cloud
An a'ni, my cloud
An an i'ah, Jah's cloud
An an i'as, Greek form of Hananiah
A'nath, afflicted: answered
An ath'e ma, accursed
An'a thoth, affliction: answers
An'drew, manly
An dro ni'cus, victory of man
A'nem, double fountain
A'ner, a lamp swept away
A neth'o thite, patronymic of Anathoth
A ni'am, lament of the people
A'nim, fountains
An'na, Greek form of Hannah
An'nas, Greek form of Hananiah
An'ti och, driven against
An'ti pas, against all: against fatherland
An ti pa'tris, against (or instead of) one's country
An to thi'jah, answers (or afflictions) of Jah
An'to thite, patronymic of Anathoth
A'nub, clustered
A pel'les, without receptacle (hide): from Greece
A phar'sa chites, as causers of division (?)

A phar'sath chites, I will divide the deceivers (?)
A phar'sites, causers of division (?)
A'phek, restrained
A phe'kah, restraint
Aph i'ah, I will make to breathe
A'phik, channel: restraint
Aph'rah, dust-heap
Aph'ses (the), the shattering
Ap ol lo'ni a, utter destruction
Ap ol'los, destroyer
Ap ol'ly on, destroyer
Ap pa'im, double-nosed
Ap'phi a, dear one
Ap pi i fo'rum, persuasive mart
A quil'a { I shall be nourished (if from Hebrew)
an eagle (if Latin)
immovable (if Greek)
Ar, awaking
A'ra, I shall see (?)
A'rab, an ambush
Ar'ab ah (the), the desert plain
A ra'bi a, dusky: mixed
A ra'bi ans, gentilic of preceding
A'rad, wild ass
A'rah, a wayfarer (literally, he wandered)
A'ram, exalted
A ram i'tess, probably feminine gentilic of preceding, but exact for the exalted of Jah.
A'ram na ha ra'im, highland of the two rivers
A'ram zo'bah, exalted station: exalted conflict
A'ran, a wild goat: I shall shout for joy
Ar'a rat, the curse reversed: precipitation of curse
A rau'nah, I shall shout for joy
A rau'nah (2), make ye to shine (in 2 Sam. 24: 16 — but most consider it an error for preceding.)
A rau'nah (3), joyful shouting of Jah (in 2 Sam. 24: 18)
Ar'ba, four
Ar'bah, four

Ar′bath ite (the), gentilic of Beth-arabah
Ar′bel, see Beth-arbel
Ar′bite, gentilic of Arab
Ar che la′us, ruling the people
Ar′che vites, plural of following
Ar′chi (the), lengthy: gentilic of Erech
Ar chip′pus, horse chief
Ar′chite (the), see Archi
Arc′tu rus, consuming (appellative for moth)
Ard, I shall subdue
Ard′ites, gentilic of preceding
Ar′don, subduer: fugitive
A re′li, a lion is my God: he cursed my God
A re′lites, gentilic of preceding
Ar e op′a gite, gentilic of following
A re op′ag us, a martial peak
Ar e′tas, virtuous
Ar′gob, lion's den; clod-heap: cursed heap
A rid′a i, the lion is enough
A rid′a tha, the lion of the decree
A ri′eh (the), the lion
A′ri el, lion of God
A rim a the′a, a high place (from same as Ramah)
A′ri och, lion-like
A ris′a i, lion of my banners (?)
Ar is tar′chus, best ruler
A ris to bu′lus, best counsellor
Ark′ite, my gnawing
Ar ma ged′don, hill of slaughter
Ar me′ni a, same as Ararat
Ar mo′ni, my palace
Ar′nan, lion of perpetuity: or same as Aran
Ar′non, lion of perpetuity: I shall shout for joy
A′rod, I shall subdue: I shall roam
Ar′o di, perhaps patronymic of preceding
A′rod ites, patronymic of Arod
A ro′er, destitute
A ro′er ite, gentilic of preceding

Ar'pad, I shall be spread out (or supported)

Ar'phad, I shall be spread out (or supported)

Ar phax'ad, I shall fail as the breast: he cursed the breast-bottle

Ar tax erx'es, { I will make the spoiled to boil / I will stir myself (in) winter

Ar tax erx'es, { I will make the sixth to boil / I will stir myself (with) drink

Ar'te mas, safe and sound

Ar'u both, windows

A ru'mah, I shall be exalted

Ar'vad, I shall break loose

Ar'vad ites, gentilic of preceding

Ar'za, earthiness

A'sa, healer: injurious (?)

As'a hel, wrought of God

As a hi'ah, wrought of Jah

As a i'ah, same as preceding

A'saph, a gatherer

A sar'e el, I shall be prince of God

As a re'lah, guided towards God

A'se nath, I shall be hated: she has stored up

A'ser, Greek form of Asher

A'shan, smoke

Ash be'a, I shall make to swear

Ash'bel, a man in God: a man of Baal: fire of Bel: I will make a path

Ash'bel ite, patronymic of preceding

Ash'che naz, a man as sprinkled: fire as scattered

Ash'dod, I will spoil

Ash'dod ites, gentilic of preceding

Ash'doth ites, same as preceding

Ash'doth pis'gah, spoilers of the survey

Ash'er, happy

Ash'er ah, groves (for idol worship)

Ash'er ites, patronymic of Asher

Ash'i ma, guiltiness: I will make desolate

Ash'ke lon, the fire of infamy: I shall be weighed

Ash'ke naz, same as Ashchenaz

Ash'nah, I will cause change

Ash'pe naz, I will make prominent the sprinkled

Ash'ri el, I shall be prince of God

Ash'ta roth, plural of following

Ash'ter ath ite, gentilic of Ashtaroth

Ash'ter oth kar na'im, double-horned mind readers: double-horned flocks

Ash'to reth, thought searching

Ash'ur, I shall be early sought: I shall be black: fire-hole.

Ash'ur ites, guided: blessed

Ash'vath, sleek: shiny: thoughtful: searched out

A'sia, slime: mire

A'si el, wrought of God

As'ke lon, same as Ashkelon

As'nah, same as Asenath

As nap'per, horned bull: thorn abolished

As'pa tha, the enticed gathered

As'ri el, I shall be prince of God

As'ri el ites, patronymic of preceding

Assh'ur, a step

Assh'u rim, plural of preceding

As'sir, prisoner

As'sos, nearer

As'sur, same as Asshur

As syr'i a, a step

As syr'i an, gentilic of preceding

As'ta roth, same as Ashtaroth

A sup'pim, the gatherings

A syn'cri tus, incomparable

A'tad, bramble

At'a rah, a crown

At'a roth, crowns

At'a roth a'dar, crowns of glory

At'a roth ad'dar, same as preceding

A'ter, binder: left-handed (*i.e.,* *shut* as to the right hand)

A'thach, thy due season

Ath a i'ah, Jah's due season

Ath a li'ah, due season for Jah

A the′ni ans, gentilic of Athens
Ath′ens, uncertainty
Ath′lai, my due times
At′roth shoph′an, crowns of their rapine
At′tai, my due seasons
At ta li′a, gentle father
Au gus′tus, radiant (in Luke 2: 1 only)
Au gus′tus, venerable
A′va, perverted
A′ven, perverseness
A′vim, perverters
A′vims, perverters
A′vites, perverters
A′vith, overturning
A′zal, proximity: he has reserved
Az a li′ah, reserved of Jehovah
Az a ni′ah, heard of Jah
A zar′a el, helped of God
A zar′e el, helped of God
Az a ri′ah, helped of Jah (Jehovah)
A′zaz, the strong one
A za′ zel, goat of departure
Az a zi′ah, strengthened of Jehovah
Az′buk, strong emptier
A ze′kah, fenced round: dug over
A′zel, reserved
A′zem, strenuous: bone: self-same
Az′gad, a mighty troop: strength of Gad
A′zi el, strength of God
A zi′za, mightiness
Az ma′veth, strength of death
Az′mon, the mighty
Az′noth ta′bor, ears thou wilt purge
A′zor, Greek form of Azzur
A zo′tus, Greek form of Ashdod
Az′ri el, my help is God
Az ri′kam, my help has arisen
A zu′bah, a forsaking

A'zur, helped
Az'zah, she was strong
Az'zan, their strength: strong one
Az'zur, helped

Ba'al (the), the lord (as master, owner)
Ba'al ah, mistress
Ba'al ath, mistressship
Ba'al ath be'er, mistress of the well
Ba'al be'rith, lord of the covenant
Ba'al e, lords of (Judah)
Ba al gad', lord of Gad
Ba al ha'mon, lord of the multitude
Ba al ha'nan, Baal is gracious: lord of grace
Ba al ha'zor, lord of the court: lord of trumpeting
Ba al her'mon, lord of hermon
Ba'a li, my lord
Ba'al im, the lords (idols)
Ba'al is, lord of the banner: in causing the joy
Ba al me'on, lord of the dwelling
Ba al pe'or, lord of the opening
Ba al pe ra'zim, lord of the breaches
Ba al sha li'sha, lord of the third part (triad)
Ba'al ta'mar, lord of the palm
Ba al ze'bub, lord of the fly
Ba al ze'phon, lord of the north
Ba'a na, ⎫
Ba'a nah, ⎬ in the affliction
Ba'a ra, she hath kindled: brutishness
Ba a sei'ah, in the work of Jah
Ba'a sha, in the consumption: in the haste
Ba'bel, confusion (by mixing)
Bab'y lon, confusion (by mixing)
Bab'y lo'ni ans, gentilic of preceding
Bab y lo'nish, same as Shinar
Ba'ca, the weeper
Bach'rite, patronymic of Becher
Ba ha'rum ite, gentilic of Bahurim

Ba hu'rim, choice youths
Bai'ther, division (in LXX of Josh. 15: 59)
Ba'jith (the), the house
Bak bak'kar, diligent investigator (?)
Bak'buk, a bottle (from its *gurgling*)
Bak buk i'ah, Jah's bottle: emptying of Jah
Ba'la am, swallower of the people: confounding the people
Ba'lac, Greek form of Balak
Bal'a dan, not a lord
Ba'lah, waxed old
Ba'lak, waster
Ba'mah, a high place (for idols)
Ba'moth, plural of preceding
Ba'moth Ba'al, high places of Baal
Ba'ni, my building
Ba rab'bas, son of father
Bar'ach el, blessed of God
Bar ach i'as, same as Berechiah
Ba'rak, lightning
Bar'hu mite, son of the blackened: in the pitied
Ba ri'ah, fugitive: crooked: bar (as *crossing*)
Bar je'sus, son of Jesus
Bar jo'na, son of a dove
Bar'kos, the son cut off
Bar'na bas, son of prophecy: son of consolation
Bar'sa bas, son of the host
Bar thol'o mew, son of Talmai
Bar ti mae'us, son of one esteemed: son of one unclean
Ba'ruch, blessed
Bar zil'la i, my irons: he of iron
Ba'shan (the), the shame of them: the fertile: the one in sleep
Ba'shan ha'voth ja'ir, see Havoth-jair
Bash'e math, same as Basmath
Bas'math, spice
Bath rab'bim, daughter of many
Bath she'ba, daughter of the oath
Bath shu'a, daughter of crying: daughter of opulence
Ba'vai, my goings

Baz'lith, stripping
Baz'luth, stripping
Bdel'li um, in turbidity
Be al i'ah, possessed of Jah: mastered of Jah
Be a'loth, mistresses
Beb'a i, my cavities
Be'cher, a dromedary: first-born
Be cho'rath, firstling
Be'dad, solitary
Be'dan, in judging
Be de'iah, isolated of Jah
Be el i'a da, lord of knowledge
Be el'ze bub, lord of the dwelling
Be'er, a well
Be e'ra, a well
Be e'rah, a well
Be er e'lim, well of the gods (*i.e.* mighty ones)
Be e'ri, my well
Be er la hai'ro i, well of the living (one) seeing me
Be e'roth, wells
Be e'roth ite, gentilic of preceding
Be er she'ba, well of the oath
Be esh'te rah, in Ashtoreth: in her flock
Be he'moth, beasts
Bel, lord
Be'la, swallowing
Be'lah, swallowing
Be'la ites, patronymic of preceding
Be'li al, worthlessness
Bel shaz'zar, lord of whose treasure: lord of destruction strait-
    ened
Bel te shaz'zar, lord of the straitened's treasure
Ben, a son
Ben ai'ah, built of Jehovah
Ben am'mi, son of my people
Be ne be'rak, sons of lightning
Be ne ja'ak an, sons of one who will oppress them
Ben ha'dad, son of the lot-caster: son of the shouter

Ben ha'il, son of valor
Ben ha'nan, son of the gracious giver
Ben i'nu, son of us
Ben'ja min, son of the right hand
Ben'jam ite, patronymic of preceding
Be'no, son of him
Ben o'ni, son of my sorrow
Ben zo'heth, son of releasing
Be'on, in the dwelling: indwelling
Be'or, a burning
Be'ra, in the evil
Ber a'chah, a blessing
Ber a chi'ah, blessed of Jehovah
Ber a i'ah, created of Jah
Be re'a, the pierced: the beyónd
Ber e chi'ah, blessed of Jehovah
Be'red, hail
Be'ri, my well: of the well
Be ri'ah, in evil
Be ri'ites, patronymic of preceding
Be'rites, gentilic of Beri
Be'rith, covenant
Ber ni'ce, bear thou victory
Be'ro dach bal'a dan, the causer of oppression is not a lord
Be ro'thah, place of wells
Be ro'thai, my wells
Be'ro thite, patronymic of preceding
Ber'yl, she will impoverish
Be'sai, my treaders down
Bes o dei'ah, in Jah's secret
Be'sor, good tidings
Be'tah, security
Be'ten, the belly (womb)
Beth ab'ar a, ferry-house
Beth'a nath, house of response (or affliction)
Beth'a noth, house of responses (or afflictions)
Beth'a ny, house of affliction (or response)
Beth ar'a bah (the), the desert house

Beth a'ram (the), the house of the exalted: the house of their
    hill
Beth ar'bel, house of God's ambush
Beth a'ven, house of vanity
Beth az ma'veth, house of the strength of death
Beth ba al me'on, house of the lord of the dwelling
Beth bar'ah, house of eating: house of choice
Beth bir'e i, house of my creator
Beth'car, house of the lamb: house of pasture
Beth da'gon, house of the fish (god)
Beth dib la tha'im, house of the double fig-cake
Beth'el, house of God
Beth'el ite, gentilic of preceding
Beth e'mek (the), the valley-house
Be'ther, division
Beth es'da, house of mercy
Beth e'zel, the neighbor's house: the next house
Beth ga'der, house of the wall
Beth ga'mul, house of the weaned: house of recompense
Beth hac'cer em, the vineyard-house
Beth ha'ran, house of their mount: house of the joyful shouter
Beth hog'la, same as following
Beth hog'lah, house of the languished feast
Beth ho'ron, consumer's house: cavernous house
Beth jesh'im oth, house of the wastes
Beth jes'i moth, house of the wastes
Beth leb' a oth, house of lionesses
Beth'le hem, house of bread
Beth le hem Eph'ra ta, see Ephrata
Beth'le hem ite, gentilic of Bethlehem
Beth'le hem Ju'dah, see Judah
Beth ma'a chah, house of oppression
Beth mar'ca both (the), the chariot-house
Beth me'on, house of habitation (see Baal-meon)
Beth nim'rah, house of the leopardess
Beth pa'let, house of escape
Beth paz'zez, house of dispersion
Beth pe'or, house of the opening

Beth pha'ge, green fig-house

Beth phe'let, same as Bethpalet

Beth ra'pha, house of the healer: house of the giant: house of the feeble

Beth re'hob, house of the broad way

Beth sai'da, house of provision: house of hunting

Beth'shan, house of the sharpener; perhaps variation of following

Beth she'an, house of quiet

Beth she'mesh, house of the sun

Beth'shem ite, gentilic of preceding

Beth shit'tah (the), the acacia house: house of the scourge

Beth tap'pu ah, the apple-house: house of the breather

Beth u'el, point ye out God: wasting of God

Beth'ul, separated

Beth'zur, house of the rock

Be to'nim, cavities: (pistachio) nuts

Be u'lah, married

Be'zai, my fine linen (garments)

Be zal'e el, in God's shade

Be'zek, lightning

Be'zer, munition

Bich'ri, be thou first (born)

Bid'kar, in stabbing

Big'tha, in the wine-press

Big'than, in their wine-press

Big tha'na, in their wine-press

Big'va i, in my bodies

Bil'dad, confusing (by mingling) love

Bil'e am, same as Balaam

Bil'gah, cheerfulness

Bil'ga i, my comforts

Bil'hah, in languishing: decrepitude

Bil'han, their decrepitude

Bil'shan, in slander

Bim'hal, in circumcision: in weakness (by mixture)

Bin'e a, in wandering

Bin'nu i, built up

Bir'sha, in wickedness
Bir za'vith, in leanness: choice olive
Bish'lam, in peace
Bith i'ah, daughter of Jah
Bith'ron (the), the division
Bi thyn'i a, violent rushing
Biz joth'jah, among Jah's olives
Biz'tha, booty
Blas'tus, a sprout
Bo an er'ges, sons of thunder
Bo'az, in him is strength
Boch'e ru, the first-born is he: his first-born
Bo'chim (the), the weepers
Bo'han, thumb
Bo'oz, Greek form of Boaz
Bos'cath, same as Bozkath
Bo'sor, Greek form of Beor: perhaps Ox-hill
Bo'zez, surpassing white: glistening
Boz'kath, a swelling (as of dough)
Boz'rah, a fold
Buk'ki, emptied out
Buk ki'ah, emptied out by Jehovah
Bul, increase: produce
Bu'nah, understanding
Bun'ni, I am built
Buz, contempt
Buz'i, my contempt
Buz'ite, patronymic of Buz

Cab'bon, as the prudent: as the builder
Ca'bul, as if nothing: fettered
Cae'sar, severed
Caes a re'a, derivative of preceding
Caes a re'a Phi lip'pi, composed of preceding and Philippi
Ca'ia phas, as comely
Cain, maker: fabricator (literally smith)
Cai'nan, their smith
Ca'lah, full age

Cal'a mus, sweet stalk: reed
Cal'col, nourished: comprehended
Ca'leb, a dog: whole-hearted
Ca'leb Eph'ra tah, see Caleb and Ephratah
Cal'neh, the wail is complete
Cal'no, his perfection
Cal'va ry, a skull
Ca'mon, rising up: standing
Ca'na, zealous: acquired
Ca'na an, a trafficker
Ca'na an ite, gentilic of preceding
Ca'na an ite (in N. T.), gentilic of Cana
Ca'naan i tess, feminine of Canaanite (1)
Can da'ce, possibly a sting
Can'neh, to give a flattering title
Ca per'na um, village of comfort
Caph'thor im, see Caphtorim
Caph'tor, as if to interpret: knop: he bowed down to spy out
Caph' to rim, masculine plural of preceding
Cap pa do'ci a, branded unreal
Car'bun cle, I will kindle (only in Isa. 54: 12)
Car'bun cle (2), lightning stone: (literally she shot forth)
Car'cas, as the bound (one)
Car che'mish, the head (or lamb) as if departed
Ca re'ah, bald-head
Car'mel, fruitful field
Car'mel ite, gentilic of preceding
Car'mel i tess, feminine of preceding
Car'mi, my vineyard
Car'mites, patronymic of preceding
Car'pus, fruit
Car she'na, change thou the lamb (or head, or pasture)
Ca siph'i a, longing of Jah: silver of Jah
Cas lu'him, as forgiven ones
Cas'tor (and Pollux), Jupiter's twins
Ce'dron, dark: turbid
Cen'chre a, granular: millet-like
Ce'phas, a stone

Chal ced'o ny, copper-like: flower-like
Chal'col, same as Calcol
Chal de'a, as clod-breakers
Chal de'ans, gentilic of preceding
Chal'dees, same as preceding
Cha'na an, same as Canaan
Chap'men, the search-men
Char'a shim, craftsmen
Char'che mish, same as Carchemish
Char'ran, Greek form of Haran
Che'bar, as if made clear; abundant: vehement
Ched or la o'mer, as binding for the sheaf: generation of a handful
Che'lal, complete
Chel'lu, determine ye him: consume ye him
Che'lub, a basket: a coop
Che lu'bai, my baskets
Chem'a rims, as changed ones
Che'mosh, as if departing: as if feeling
Che na'a nah, traffic: as if afflicted
Chen' a ni, as my perpetuator
Chen a ni'ah, as perpetuated of Jah
Che'phar ha am'mo nai, the covert of the Ammonites: village of the Ammonites
Che phi'rah, a young lioness: covert
Che'ran, as shouting for joy: their lamb: their pasture
Cher'eth ims, cutters off
Che'rith, a cutting
Cher'eth ites, same as Cherethims
Cher'ub, as if contending
Cher'u bim-s, masculine plural of preceding
Ches'a lon, foolish confidence: as extolled
Che'sed, as harrower
Che'sil, a fool: Orion
Che sul'loth, as raised ways: foolish confidences
Che'zib, as flowing; falsified
Chi'don, a spear: shield: dart
Chil'e ab, sustained of father

Chil′i on, consumption
Chil′mad, as a disciple: complete clothing (or measure)
Chim′ham, their longing
Chim′han, their longing (feminine)
Chin′ne reth, a harp
Chin′ne roth, harps
Chi′os, an unlucky throw of dice
Chis′leu, his confidence
Chis′lon, confidence: foolishness
Chis′loth Ta′bor, foolish confidences thou wilt purge
Chit′tim, breakers in pieces
Chi′un, an image: pillar (as *set up*)
Chlo′e, verdant
Cho ra′shan, a furnace of smoke
Cho ra′zin, probably Greek for preceding
Cho ze′ba, falsehood
Christ, the anointed
Chris′ti an, derivative of preceding (*one like* the anointed)
Chry′so lyte, gold-stone
Chry so pra′sus, golden green: golden achievement
Chub, clustered: a horde
Chun, established
Chu′shan rish a tha′im, blackness of double wickedness
Chu′za, a mound: a measure
Ci li′ci a, hair cloth
Cin′ne roth, same as Chinneroth
Cis, Greek form of Kish
Clau′da, surging (?)
Clau′di a, feminine of following
Clau′di us, whining (?): perhaps derivative of Clauda
Clau′di us lys′i as, see Lucius
Clem′ent, vine-twig: merciful
Cle′o pas, famed of all
Cle′o phas, my exchanges (another mode of writing Alpheus, should be spelled Clopas)
Cni′dus (*nidus*), nettled
Col ho′zeh, all-seer: every seer
Co los′se, monstrosities

Co los'si ans, gentilic of preceding
Con a ni'ah, established of Jehovah
Co ni'ah, Jehovah has established
Con o ni'ah, same as Conaniah
Co'os, a public prison
Co'ral, heights
Co're, Greek form of Korah
Cor'inth, satiated
Co rin'thi ans, gentilic of preceding
Cor ne'li us, pitiless satiety: pertaining to a horn
Co'sam, divining (?)
Coz, a thorn
Coz'bi, my lie
Cres'cens, growing: fleshy shadow
Crete, fleshy
Cretes,
Cre'tians, } gentilic of preceding
Cris'pus, crisp: curly-haired: seed of a ram (?)
Cush, black: terror
Cu'shan, their blackness
Cush'i, gentilic of preceding
Cuth, crushing
Cuth'ah, place of crushing
Cy'prus, love: a blossom
Cy re'ne, supremacy of the bridle (?)
Cy re'ni an, gentilic of preceding
Cy re'ni us, derivative of preceding
Cy'rus, possess thou the furnace

Dab'a reh, pasture
Dab'ba sheth, hump (of a camel): or more probably, he whispered shame
Dab'e rath, same as Dabareh
Da'gon, the fish-god (from its *fecundity*)
Dal a i'ah, drawn of Jah
Dal ma nu'tha, slow firebrand (if Greek): poor portion (if Hebrew)
Dal ma'ti a, a priestly robe (?)

Dal'phon, the weeper (?)

Dam'a ris, a yoke-bearing wife

Dam'as cenes', Greek form of gentilic of following

Da mas'cus, silent is the sackcloth weaver

Da mas'cus, sackcloth (weaver) is going about (or dwelling) (N.B., this form is in the margin Darmesek)

Dan, judging: a judge

Dan'i el, my judge is God

Dan'ites, patronymic of Dan

Dan ja'an, the judge will afflict: the judge is greedy

Dan'nah, thou hast judged: judgment

Da'ra, the arm: some read as following

Dar'da, he compassed knowledge: dwelling of knowledge

Da ri'us, investigation: the dwelling will be full of heaviness

Dar'kon, the dwelling of lamentation

Da'than, their law: their decree

Da'vid, beloved

De'bir, an oracle

Deb'o rah, a bee: her speaking

De cap'o lis, ten cities: the ten-city (region)

De'dan, their love: their moving: their proceeding

De'dan, same as preceding, with locative ending occurs only in Ez. 25: 13

De da'nim, gentilic of Dedan

De'ha vites, the sickly

De'kar, the piercer

Del a i'ah, drawn of Jah

De li'lah, brought low

De'mas, of the people: popular

De me'tri us, of mother earth

Der'be, tanner: treader of skin: coverer with skin

Deu'el, know ye God

Dia'mond, he will smite down

Di an'a, complete light: flow restrained

Dib'la im, the double fig-cake

Dib'lath, place of the fig-cake

Dib la tha'im, feminine of Diblaim.

Dib'on, the waster: sufficient understanding (?)

Di'bon Gad, see Gad
Dib'ri, my word
Did'y mus, double, *i.e.,* a twin
Dik'lah, date palm: the beaten-small fainted
Dil'e an, the emptied beclouded (?): brought low in affliction
Dim'nah, dung hill
Di'mon, the quieter: silence
Di mo'nah, feminine of preceding: sufficient numbering
Di'nah, judgment
Di'na ites, gentilic of preceding
Din'ha bah, give thou judgment
Di o ny'sius, devotee of Bacchus: devotee of the wine-press: or
    perhaps " divinely pricked "
Di ot're phes, Jove-nourished
Di'shan, their threshing: their treading
Di'shon, a thresher: the pygarg
Diz'a hab, sufficiency of gold
Do'da i, my loves
Do da'nim, their loves (?)
Do da'vah, beloved of Jehovah
Do'do, his beloved
Do'eg, fearful
Doph'kah, beating (literally, thou hast beaten)
Dor, generation: dwelling
Dor'cas, a gazelle
Do'than, double decree: double sickness (Gen. 37: 17)
Do'than, their decree: their sickness
Dru sil'la, dewy (?)
Du'mah, silence
Du'ra, habitation

East'er, the passover
E'bal, heaps of nothing: heaps of confusion
E'bed, servant
E'bed me'lech, servant of the king
Eb en e'zer, the stone of help
E'ber, beyond: the other side (as having *crossed over*)
E bi'a saph, father is adder

Eb ro'na, crossing place
Ec cle si as'tes, the convoker: the preacher
Ed, a witness
E'dar, a flock
E'den, delight
E'der, a flock
E'dom, red
E'dom ites, gentilic of Edom
Ed're i, goodly pasture
Eg'lah, a heifer
Eg la'im, double reservoir
Eg'lon, a bull calf
E'gypt, double straits
E gyp'tians, gentilic of Egypt
E'hi, my brother
E'hud, undivided: union (1 Ch. 8: 6)
E'hud (2), I will give thanks: I will be praised
E'ker, an offshoot: eradication
Ek'ron, uprooting
Ek'ron ite, gentilic of preceding
El'a dah, God has adorned
E'lah, a terebinth: an oak
E'lam, their heaps: suckling them: eternal
E'lam ites, gentilic of Elam
El'a sah, God has wrought
E'lath, mightiness: terebinth
El beth'el, God of God's house
El da'ah, God has known
El'dad, God has loved
E'le ad, God is witness
El e a'leh, God is ascending
El e'a sah, same as Elasah
El e a'zar, God is helper
El e lo'he is'ra el, God the God of Israel
El'eph, a thousand: a disciple
El ha'nan, God is a gracious giver
E'li, my God
E'li (2), elevated (high priest in Samuel's time)

E li'ab, my God is father

E li'a da,
E li'a dah, } God is knower

E li'ah, my God is Jah

E li'ah ba, God will hide

E li'a kim, God will establish

E li'am, God of the people

E li'as, Greek form of Elijah

E li'a saph, God is adder

E li'a shib, God will restore

E li'a thah, God of the coming (one)

E li'dad, my God is lover

E'li el, God of might: my God is El (*i.e.*, God)

E li e'nai, God of my eyes

E li e'zer, God of help

E li ho e'na i, unto Jehovah mine eyes

E li ho'reph, God of winter (harvest-time)

E li'hu, God of him: my God is Jehovah

E li'jah, my God is Jehovah

E li'ka, my God has spued out

E'lim, mighty ones

E lim'e lech, my God is king

E li o e'na i, unto Jehovah mine eyes

El'i phal, my God has judged

E liph'a let, God of escape

El'i phaz, God of fine gold: my God has refined

E liph'e leh, my God, set thou apart: God of his distinction

E liph'e let, God of escape

E lis'a beth, Greek form of Elisheba

El i se'us, Greek form of Elisha

E li'sha, my God is salvation

E li'shah, my God has disregarded

E lish'a ma, my God is a hearer

E lish'a phat, my God is judge

E lish'e ba, God of the oath (or seven)

E lish'u a, God of supplication: God of opulence

E li'ud, God of majesty

E liz'a phan, my God is hider

E li'zur, my God is a rock
El ka'nah, God has purchased
El'ko shite, of the gathered of God
El la'sar, God is chastener
El mo'dam, possibly Greek for Almodad
El na'am, God is delight
El na'than, God is a giver
E'lo i, my God
E'lon, might: see Elah and Elath; terebinth: plain
E'lon beth ha'nan, might of the house of the gracious giver
E'lon ites, patronymic of Elon
E'lon za an an'nim, power of the demolitions: see Zaanannim
E'loth, mightinesses: terebinths
El pa'al, God is maker
El pa'let, God is escape
El pa'ran, the power of their adorning
El te'keh, let God spue thee out
El te'kon, made straight of God
El to'lad, may God cause thee to beget
E'lul, nothingness
E lu'za i, God is my gathering strength (for flight)
El'y mas, wise: learned: a magician
El za'bad, God is endower
El za'phan, God is hider (layer up)
Em'er ald, enameled
E'mims, terror
Em man'u el, with us is God
Em'ma us, in earnest longing
Em'mor, an ass
E'nam, their fountain
E'nan, their fountain (feminine)
En'dor, fountain of the dwelling
E ne'as, uttering praise
En eg la'im, fountain of the two calves
En gan'nim, fountain of gardens
En ge'di, fountain of the kid
En had'dah, fountain of joy: fount of sharpening
En hak'ko re, fount of the caller

En ha'zor, fountain of the village: fount of trumpeting
En mish'pat, fount of judgment
E'noch, dedicated
E'nos, (mortal) man
E'nosh, same as preceding correctly spelled
En rim'mon, fount of the pomegranate
En ro'gel, fount of the spy
En she'mesh, fount of the sun
En tap'pu ah, fount of the apple (*i.e.,* the breather)
E pæn'e tus, same as Epenetus
Ep'aph ras, foam-covered; or possibly contraction of following
E paph ro di'tus, lovely: fascinating
Ep e ne'tus, praiseworthy
E'phah, darkness
E'phai, my coverings: my shadows: my fowls
E'pher, dustiness
E'phes dam'mim, limit of bloods
E phe'sian, gentilic of following
Eph'e sus, full purposed: a throwing at
Eph'lal, I shall intercede (or judge)
E'phod, a (special) girdle
Eph'pha tha, I shall be opened
E'phra im, double ash-heap: I shall be doubly fruitful
E'phra im ite-s, patronymic of preceding
E'phra in, doubly dust
Eph'ra tah, ash-heap: place of fruitfulness
Eph'rath, ashiness: fruitfulness
Eph'rath ite, gentilic of preceding
E'phron, he of dust
E pi cu re'an, a helper: defender
Er, awaking: stirring up
E'ran, their awaking: their stirring up
E'ran ites, patronymic of preceding
E ras'tus, beloved
E'rech, long
E'ri, my awaking: my stirring up
E'rites, patronymic of preceding
E sa'i as, Greek form of Isaiah

E sar had'don, captivity of the fierce: I will chastise the fierce
E'sau, shaggy: his doings
E'sek, strife
Esh'ba al, man of Baal: fire of Baal
Esh'ban, fire of discernment
Esh'col, a cluster
Esh'e an, I will rely (lean)
E'shek, oppression
Esh'ka lon ites, gentilic of Ashkelon
Esh'ta ol, I will be entreated
Esh'ta ul ites, gentilic of preceding
Esh te mo'a, I will make myself heard
Esh'te moh, I shall cause my own ruin: fire of astonishment: I
    shall soar aloft
Esh'ton, effeminate
Es'li, perhaps Greek for Azaliah
Es'rom, perhaps Greek for Hezron
Es'ther, I will be hidden
E'tam, their ravening
E'tham, with them: their plowshare
E'than, strength: perpetuity
Eth'a nim, plural of preceding
Eth ba'al, with Baal
E'ther, entreaty: abundance
E thi o'pia, black
E thi o'pi an, gentilic of preceding
Eth'nan, hire of unchastity
Eth'ni, my hire
Eu bu'lus, of good counsel
Eu ni'ce, well-won: (literally happy victory)
Eu o'di as, a sweet smell; a good journey
Eu phra'tes, fruitfulness
Eu roc'ly don, an easterly tempest
Eu'ty chus, well off
Eve, life giver
E'vi, my desire
E vil me ro'dach, foolish is thy rebellion
E'zar, treasure

Ez'ba i, my humblings (?)
Ez'bon, hasting to discern: I will be enlargement
E ze ki'as, Greek for Hezekiah
E ze'ki el, he will be strengthened of God
E'zel, departure
E'zem, same as Azem
E'zer, same as Ezar (only in Gen. 36, and 1 Ch. 1: 42)
E'zer (2), an help
E'zi on ga'ber, counsel of a man: backbone of a man
E'zi on ge'ber, same as preceding
Ez'nite, the stiff-backed
Ez'ra, help
Ez'ra hite, a native (as *arising* out of the soil)
Ez'ri, my help

Fair ha'vens, goodly ports
Fe'lix, delusive: happy (if Latin)
Fes'tus, told out: festal
For tu na'tus, well freighted
Frank in'cense, whiteness

Ga'al, loathing
Ga'ash, shaking
Ga'ba, elevation
Gab'ba i, my eminences: my convexities
Gab'ba tha, the high place
Ga'bri el, man of God (*i.e.*, man in the sense of *prevailer*)
Gad, an invader: a troop: fortune
Gad a renes', reward at the end (meaning of best supported reading)
Gad'di, my invader: my troop: my fortune
Gad'di el, my fortune is God
Ga'di, same as following
Gad'ites, patronymic of Gad
Ga'ham, the valley was lost: the devastator waxed hot
Ga'har, the valley burned
Ga'ius, on earth
Ga'lal, a roller (*i.e.*, one who rolls): because of

Ga la'tia, milky (?)
Ga la'tians, gentilic of preceding
Gal ba'num, the best (*i.e.*, the fat) lamenting: a fortress built
Gal'e ed, a heap of witness
Gal i læ'an-s, same as Galileans
Gal i le'an-s, gentilic of Galilee
Gal'i lee, a circuit (as *enclosed*, or *rolled around*)
Gal'lim, billows (as *heaps* of water)
Gal'li o, a priest of Cybele: an eunuch (?)
Gam a'li el, my recompenser is God
Gam'ma dims, cutters: additional garments
Ga'mul, weaned: recompensed
Ga'reb, scabby
Gar'mite, bony (as *strong*)
Gash'mu, his rain
Ga'tam, reach thou the end: their touch
Gath, a wine-press
Gath heph'er, see Hepher
Gath rim'mon, wine-press of the pomegranate
Ga'za, she was strong
Ga'zath ites, gentilic of Gaza
Ga'zer, a piece: portion (cut off)
Ga'zez, shearer
Ga'zites, same as Gazathites
Gaz'zam, palmer-worm — literally their shearing
Ge'ba, same as Gaba
Ge'bal, a boundary
Ge'ber, a man (as mighty), see Gabriel
Ge'bim, ditches: beams: locusts
Ged a li'ah, magnified of Jehovah
Ged'e on, Greek for Gideon
Ge'der, a wall
Ged'e rah, a fold (for sheep)
Ged'e rath ite, gentilic of Geder
Ged'e rite, same as preceding
Ged'e roth, sheep-cotes
Ged er oth a'im, double sheep-cote
Ge'dor, the walling in

Ge ha'zi, valley of my vision
Ge hen'na, hell (from " the valley of Hinnom," see Hinnom)
Gel'il oth, circles: borders
Ge mal'li, my camel: *camelish*
Gem a ri'ah, completed of Jah
Gen'e sis, generation: beginning
Gen nes'a ret, Greek for Chinnereth
Gen'tiles, nations
Ge nu'bath, theft
Ge'ra, the cud: a grain: sojourning
Ge'rah, one twentieth of a shekel
Ge'rar, dragging away: ruminating: sojourning
Ger ge senes', probably Greek for Girgashites
Ger'iz im, the cutters off
Ger'shom, a stranger there: a stranger desolate
Ger'shon, an outcast
Ger'shon ites, patronymic of Gershon
Ge'sham, their clod
Ge'shem, rain
Ge'shur, proud beholder
Gesh'u ri, same as following
Gesh'ur ites, gentilic of Geshur
Ge'ther, a proud spy
Geth sem'a ne, oil-press place
Ge u'el, exalt ye God
Ge'zer, a piece: a portion (as *cut off*)
Gez'rites, gentilic of base of Gerizim.   Some copies would make
     it gentilic of Gezer
Gi'ah, to break forth
Gib'bar, the valiant
Gib'be thon, the lofty
Gib'e a, a hill
Gib'e ah, a hill
Gib'e ath, hilliness
Gib'e ath ite, gentilic of Gibeath
Gib'e on, little hill: hilly
Gib'e on ite, gentilic of preceding
Gib'lites, gentilic of Gebal

Gid dal'ti, I have magnified
Gid'del, he has magnified
Gid'e on, the cutter down
Gid e o'ni, my cutter down
Gi'dom, a cutting down
Gi'hon, the breaking forth
Gil'a lai, my rolls: my dung (as *rolled*)
Gil bo'a, boiling spring: literally rolling, pouring out
Gil'e ad, heap of witness: rolling forever
Gil'e ad ite, gentilic of preceding
Gil'gal, rolling: a wheel
Gi'loh, uncovered: stripped (as a captive)
Gi'lon ite, gentilic of preceding
Gim'zo, swallowing this: this is a rush (?)
Gi'nath, protection: a garden (as *protected*)
Gin'ne tho, his protection: his garden
Gin'neth on, protection: gardener
Gir'gash ites, a stranger drawing near (?)
Gir'gas ite, same as Girgashite
Gis'pa, the clod breathed
Git'tah he'pher, toward the wine-press of the digging
Git ta'im, the double wine-press
Git'tites, gentilic of Gath
Git'tith, feminine of preceding
Gi'zon ite, shearer: quarryman
Go'ath, lowing
Gob, a locust: a pit
Gog, to cover: surmount: top
Go'lan, their captivity: their rejoicing
Gol'go tha, a skull: place of a skull
Go li'ath, stripped (as a captive)
Go'mer, completion
Go mor'rah, bondage
Go mor'rha, same as preceding
Go'pher, coverer: pitch-wood
Go'shen, drawing near
Go'zan, their passing away
Gre'cia, unstable: the miry one — see Javan

Gre'ci an, masculine plural of preceding
Gre'ci an (in N.T.), a Hellenist, or Greek-speaking Jew
Greece, Greek for Grecia
Greek-s, gentilic of preceding
Gud go'dah, the slashing place
Gu'ni, my defender (?)
Gu'nites, patronymic of preceding
Gur, to sojourn
Gur ba'al, sojourn of Baal

Ha a hash'ta ri, gentilic of an unknown base, meaning " I will
    diligently observe the searching "
Hab a i'ah, hidden of Jah
Ha'bak kuk, ardently embraced
Hab az in i'ah, the hiding of Jah's thorn
Ha'bor, to join
Hach a li'ah, the waiting on Jah
Hach'i lah, darkness: the waiting of faintness: waiting for her
Hach'mo ni, of the wise one: I was wise
Hach'mon ite, same as preceding
Ha'dad, I shall move softly: I shall love (1 Kings 11: 17)
Ha'dad (2), noisy
Ha'dad (3), sharp (1 Ch. 1: 30)
Had ad e'zer, noisy helper
Ha dad rim'mon, sound of the pomegranate
Ha'dar, honor
Ha'dar, privy chamber (in Gen. 25: 18)
Had ar e'zer, honor of the helper
Had'a shah, renewal
Ha das'sah, the myrtle
Ha dat'tah, sharpness: newness
Ha'did, making sharp
Had'la i, my forbearings
Ha do'ram, their honor
Ha'drach, thy privy chamber
Ha'gab, locust: grasshopper
Hag'a ba, same as following
Hag'a bah, feminine of Hagab

Ha'gar, ensnaring: the sojourner
Ha gar enes', masculine plural of preceding
Ha'gar ites, same as preceding
Ha'ger ite, singular of preceding
Hag'ga i, my feasts
Hag'ge ri, same as Hagerite
Hag'gi, my feast
Hag gi'ah, a feast of Jah
Hag'gites, gentilic of Haggi
Hag'gith, festivity
Ha'i, same as Ai, with article; " the heap "
Hak'ka tan, the small
Hak'koz, the thorn
Ha ku'pha, decree of the month
Ha'lah, painful: fresh anguish
Ha'lak, smooth
Hal'hul, travail-pain
Ha'li, an ornament
Hal le lu'iah, praise ye Jah
Hal lo'hesh, the charmer
Hal o'hesh, same as preceding
Ham, tumult: he raged (in Gen. 14: 5)
Ham (2) hot (the same form is rendered " father-in-law ")
Ha'man, the rager: their tumult
Ha'math, enclosure of wrath
Ha'math ite, gentilic of preceding
Ha'math zo'bah, the swelling host's enclosure of wrath
Ham'math, hot place
Ham med'a tha, measurement
Ham'me lech, the king
Ham mol'e keth, the queen (literally, the she did reign)
Ham'mon, sunny(?): hot
Ham moth dor', hot places of the dwelling (or generation)
Ha'mon, see Baal-hamon
Ha mo'nah, multitudinous
Ha'mon gog, the multitude of Gog
Ha'mor, an ass
Ham'u el, they were heated of God

Ha'mul, pitied
Ha'mul ites, gentilic of preceding
Ha mu'tal, father-in-law of dew
Ha nam'e el, place of God's favor
Ha'nan, a gracious giver
Ha nan'e el, the grace of God
Ha na'ni, my grace: gracious
Han a ni'ah, the grace of Jah
Ha'nes, grace has fled: ensign of grace
Han'i el, favor of God
Han'nah, she was gracious
Han'na thon, graciously regarded
Han'ni el, same as Haniel
Ha'noch, dedicated
Ha'noch ites, patronymic of preceding
Ha'nun, favored
Haph ra'im, double digging
Ha'ra, mountainous
Har'a dah, fear
Ha'ran, their mountain (name of Lot's father, and of a man in
    1 Ch. 23: 9)
Ha'ran (2), their burning
Ha'ra rite, the curser (2 Sam. 23: 33)
Ha'ra rite (2) a mountaineer (patronymic of Shammah)
Ha'ra rite (3), my mountain (in 2 Sam. 23: 11)
Har bo'na, ⎱ droughtiness
Har bo'nah, ⎰
Ha'reph, reproachful: autumnal (?)
Ha'reth, the cutting (engraving)
Har ha i'ah, kindled of Jah
Har'has, he burned, he pitied
Har'hur, inflammation
Ha'rim, banned: flat-nosed
Ha'riph, reproach: autumnal
Har ne'pher, the frustrator burnt
Ha'rod, trembling
Ha'rod ites, gentilic of preceding
Ha ro'eh, the vision

Ha'ro rite, the mountaineer

Har'o sheth, carving

Har'sha, artifice: deviser: secret work

Ha'rum, the haughty one: high

Ha ru'maph, banned of nose

Ha ru'phite, patronymic of Hariph

Ha'ruz, acute: decision: maimed: decreed

Has a di'ah, shown mercy of Jah

Has e nu'ah, the thorny: the hated (this is Senuah with definite article prefixed)

Hash a bi'ah, regarded of Jehovah

Ha shab'nah, inventiveness: the device was lamented

Hash ab ni'ah, the devising of Jah

Hash bad'a na, he hasted in the judgment: considerate in the judgment

Ha'shem, to make desolate

Hash mo'nah, he hasted the numbering

Hash'ub, considerate

Hash u'bah, consideration

Ha'shum, the desolate hasted

Hash u'pha, stripped

Has'rah, she was lacking

Has'sen a'ah, the thorn-bush

Has'shub, same as Hashub

Has u'pha, same as Hashupha

Ha'tach, why wilt thou smite

Ha'thath, dismay; casting down

Ha ti'pha, seizure

Ha ti'ta, my sin removed: a digging

Hat'til, sin cast out

Hat'tush, sin was hasted

Hau'ran, their whiteness

Hav'i lah, anguish (as *travail*-pain)

Ha'voth ja'ir, villages of Jair (perhaps " producers of Jair," the first part being feminine plural of "'life," hence " lives," " living places," " producers."

Ha'za el, seen of God

Ha za i'ah, seen of Jah

Ha'zar ad'dar, enclosure of glory
Ha zar e'nan, enclosure of the one with eyes (Ezek. 47: 17)
Ha zar e'nan (2), enclosure of their fountain
Ha zar gad'dah, enclosure of conflict: enclosure of fortune
Ha zar hat'ti con, the middle enclosure
Ha zar ma'veth, enclosure of death
Ha zar shu'al, enclosure of the jackal
Ha zar su'sah, mare enclosure
Ha zar su'sim, enclosure of horses
Ha'za zon ta'mar, pruning of the palm: division of the palm
Haz'el el po'ni, the shadow turned towards me
Haz'e rim, enclosures
Haz'e roth, enclosures (feminine)
Haz'e zon ta'mar, archer of the palm tree (?): same as Hazazon-
    tamar
Ha'zi el, vision of God
Ha'zo, his vision: seen of him
Ha'zor, to trumpet: enclosure
Ha'zor had at'tah, enclosure of rejoicing: new enclosure, or pos-
    sibly " trumpeting of joy: trumpeting anew "
He'ber, a company: enchantment
He'ber (2), same as Eber (in 1 Ch. 5: 13–8: 22)
He'ber ites, patronymic of Heber (1)
He'brew-s, patronymic of Eber — an Eberite
He'brew ess, same as preceding (feminine)
He'bron, communion
He'bron (2), one who has crossed (in Josh. 19: 28)
He'bron ites, patronymic of Hebron (1)
He'ga i, my meditations
He'ge, meditation
He'lah, disease: rust: scum
He'lam, their rampart: their force
Hel'bah, fatness
Hel'bon, the fat one
Hel'da i, my times
He'leb, the fat
He'led, the age
He'lek, a portion

He'lek ites, patronymic of preceding
He'lem, smiter (in 1 Ch. 7: 35)
He'lem (2), a dream: robust
He'leph, exchange
He'lez, stripped (as for battle)
He'li, Greek for Eli
Hel'ka i, my portions
Hel'kath, a possession
Hel'kath haz zu'rim, possession of the besieger
He'lon, travail-stricken: rampart: very strong
He'mam, crushed: crusher
He'man, right-handed: faithful
He'math, same as Hammath
Hem'dan, their desire
Hen, favor: grace
He'na, the shaken
Hen'a dad, favor of Hadad
He'noch, same as Enoch and Hanoch
He'pher, a pit: shame
He'pher ites, patronymic of preceding
Heph'zi bah, my delight is in her
He'res, the sun
He'resh, an artificer
Her'mas, sand bank: the word is also Doric for following
Her'mes, bringer of good luck: teacher for gain
Her mog'e nes, lucky-born
Her'mon, devoted: banned
Her'mon ites, masculine plural and gentilic of Hermon
Her'od, heroic
He ro'di ans, gentilic of preceding
He ro'di as, feminine of Herod
He ro'di on, valiant
He'sed, mercy
Hesh'bon, device: reason
Hesh'mon, quiet reckoning (?): hasting the separation
Heth, terror
Heth'lon, swaddled
Hez'ek i, my strong (one)

Hez e ki'ah, strengthened of Jehovah

He'zi on, the vision

He'zir, swine

Hez'ra i, his enclosure

Hez'ra i (2), my enclosures (another reading in 2 Sam. 23: 35)

Hez'ro, his court (correct spelling of Hezrai (1)

Hez'ron, enclosed: arrow of song: division of song

Hez'ron ites, patronymic of preceding

Hid'da i, my noises: my echoes

Hid'de kel, riddle of the (date) palm: riddle of lightness

Hi'el, the life of God

Hi e rap'o lis, temple city

Hig ga'ion, meditation

Hi'len, pain them

Hil ki'ah, the portion of Jehovah

Hil'lel, to be praised

Hin'nom, to make self drowsy: behold them

Hi'rah, paleness: hollowness

Hi'ram, their paleness

Hit'tite-s, patronymic of Heth

Hi'vites, showers of life: livers

Hiz ki'ah ⎱ same as Hezekiah
Hiz ki'jah ⎰

Ho'bab, loving: a lover

Ho'bah, hiding: affectionate

Hod, glory

Ho da i'ah, another form of following

Ho da vi'ah, his glory is Jehovah

Ho'desh, the month (as marked by the *new moon*)

Ho de'vah, glory of Jah

Ho di'ah, ⎱ my glory is Jah
Ho di'jah, ⎰

Hog'lah, the feast has languished

Ho'ham, alas, he crushed

Ho'lon, anguished: sandy

Ho'mam, crushed

Hoph'ni, my fist: fisty

Hoph'ra, to cover evil

Hor, progenitor
Ho'ram, their progenitor
Ho'reb, a waster
Ho'rem, banned
Hor ha gid'gad, the slashing hole
Ho'ri, my cave: my whiteness: my noble: cave-ite
Ho'rims, patronymic of preceding
Ho'rites, patronymic of Hori
Hor'mah, destruction
Hor o na'im, double cave
Hor'o nite, troglodite: gentilic of preceding or of Beth-horon
Ho'sah, trusting
Ho san'nah, save, I beseech thee
Ho se'a, to save
Ho sha i'ah, saved of Jah
Ho sha'mah, Jehovah is hearer
Ho she'a, to save — same as Hosea
Ho'tham, a signet
Ho'than, incorrect spelling of preceding
Ho'thir, a surplus
Huk'kok, the law (as *graven*, or *appointed*)
Hu'kok, the engraving
Hul, to have pain
Hul'dah, a weasel: perpetuity
Hum'tah, lowliness: place of lizards
Hu'pham, their covering
Hu'pham ites, patronymic of preceding
Hup'pah, a covering
Hup'pim, coverings
Hur, a hole: white
Hu'ra i, my caves: my white (stuffs)
Hu'ram, their whiteness
Hu'ri, my whiteness: my cave
Hu'shah, haste
Hu'sha i, my hastenings
Hu'sham, their haste
Hu'shath ite, patronymic of Hushah
Hu'shim, hasters

Huz, counsellor
Huz′zab, he was established
Hy me næ′us, a wedding song

Ib′har, he will choose
Ib′le am, he will swallow them: he will swallow the people
Ib nei′ah, Jah will build
Ib ni′jah, he will be built of Jah
Ib′ri, a Hebrew (literally one who has *crossed*)
Ib′zan, their whitness (literally their *tin* — as white)
Ich′a bod, woe (where?), the glory
I co′ni um, the comer: image-like: yielding
Id′a lah, he will fly to her: hand of imprecation
Id′bash, hand of shame: honeyed
Id′do, I will praise him (Ezra 8: 17, 17–1 Ch. 27: 21)
Id′do (2), his appointment: he will adorn him (2 Ch. 9: 29)
Id′do (3), due time: adorn him
Id u mæ′a, same as following
I du me′a, same as Edom
I′gal, he will redeem
Ig da li′ah, Jehovah will wax great
Ig′e al, same as Igal
I′im, heaps (of ruins)
I je ab′a rim, heaps of the regions beyond or of " those who have
    crossed "
I′jon, ruinous
Ik′kesh, perverse
I′la í, my elevations: my sucklings
Il lyr′i cum, the lyric band (?)
Im′la, ⎱
Im′lah, ⎰ he will fulfil
Im man′u el, with us is God
Im′mer, he hath said
Im′na, he will withhold
Im′nah, right-handed: the right side: he will number
Im′rah, he will rebel
Im′ri, my saying
In′di a, flee ye away: give ye thanks

Iph e de i'ah, Jah will redeem

Ir, a city

I'ra, wakeful: a city

I'rad, a wild ass: city of witness (?)

I'ram, their city

I'ri, my city

I ri'jah, fear thou Jah: Jah will see me

Ir na'hash, city of the serpent

I'ron, tearful

Ir'pe el, God will heal

Ir she'mesh, city of the sun

I'ru, they were awake: awake ye

I'sa ac, he shall laugh

I'sa ac (2), he will laugh (in mockery) (Ps. 105: 9; Jer. 33: 26; Amos 7: 9, 16)

I sa'iah, save thou Jehovah

Is'cah, he will pour her out: he will anoint her: he will screen her

Is car'i ot, he will be hired: a man of the cities (?)

Ish'bah, he will praise

Ish'bak, he will leave (alone)

Ish bi be'nob, his dwelling is in Nob

Ish bo'sheth, man of shame

I'shi, my husband (literally " my man ") (Hos. 2: 16)

I'shi (2), my salvation

I shi'ah, Jah will lend: forgotten of Jah

I shi'jah, same as preceding

Ish'ma, desolation

Ish'ma el, God will hear

Ish'ma el ite-s, patronymic of preceding

Ish ma i'ah, Jehovah will hear

Ish'me el ites, same as Ishmaelites

Ish'me rai, they will be my keepers

I'shod, man of glory

Ish'pan, he will make them prominent: he will lay them bare

Ish'tob, good man

Ish'u ah, he shall equalize

Ish'u ai, he will justify me

Ish′u i, same as preceding

Is ma chi′ah, Jehovah will uphold

Is ma i′ah, Jah will hear

Is′pah, he will be prominent: he will lay bare

Is′ra el, he shall be prince of God

Is′ra el ites, patronymic of preceding

Is′ra el i tish, feminine of preceding

Is′sa char, he will be hired: there is reward: he will bring reward

Is shi′ah, same as Ishiah

Is′u ah, same as Ishuah

Is′u i, same as Ishuai

It al′i an, gentilic of following

It′a ly, vituline (*i.e.,* calf-like)

Ith′a i, with me

Ith′a mar, palm-coast

Ith′i el, with me is God

Ith′mah, orphanage: orphanhood

Ith′nan, he will hire them: he will stretch out

Ith′ra, abundance: excellence

Ith′ran, their abundance: their excellence

Ith′re am, abundance (or remnant) of the people

Ith′rites, patronymic of Jether

It′tah ka′zin, to the due time of the prince

It′ta i, with me

I tu ræ′a, past the limits: or possibly same as Jetur

I′vah, he is a perverter

Iz′e har, oil

Iz′e har ites, patronymic of preceding

Iz′har, same as Izehar

Iz′har ites, same as Izeharites

Iz ra hi′ah, Jah will arise (as the sun)

Iz′ra hite, he will arise

Iz′ri, my imagination: my thought

Ja′a kan, let him oppress them

Ja ak′o bah, he will seek to overreach

Ja a′la, a wild goat (as *climber*)

Ja a'lah, a wild goat (ibex)

Ja a'lam, he will hide

Ja'a nai, he will give my answers

Ja ar e or'e gim, forests of the weavers

Ja'a sau, they will make him: they will perform

Ja a'si el, it will be done of God

Ja az a ni'ah, Jehovah will give ear

Ja a'zer, let him help

Ja a zi'ah, he will be strengthened of Jehovah

Ja a'zi el, he will be strengthened of God

Ja'bal, a stream

Jab'bok, he will empty out

Ja'besh, dry

Ja'besh gil'e ad, see Gilead

Ja'bez, whiteness swept away: mire swept away: shovel of mire

Ja'bin, he will understand

Jab'ne el, God will build

Jab'neh, he will cause to build

Ja'chan, let him make trouble

Ja'chin, he will establish

Ja'chin ites, patronymic of preceding

Ja'cinth, hyacinth: blue

Ja'cob, he will take by the heel

Ja'da, the knower (*i.e.* the one who knows)

Ja'dau, my loves

Jad'du a, knowing

Ja'don, he will strive (or judge)

Ja'el, ibex (a mountain goat)

Ja'gur, he will sojourn

Jah, a contraction of Jehovah, used in the sense of Victor

Ja'hath, he will snatch away: union

Ja'haz, trodden down

Ja ha'za, }
Ja ha'zah, } to the treading down: treading down place

Ja ha zi'ah, Jah will see

Ja ha'zi el, God will cause to see

Jah'da i, whom he will place

Jah'di el, he will be gladdened of God

Jah'do, his enmity
Jah'le el, the hope of God
Jah'le el ites, patronymic of Jahleel
Jah'ma i, he will be my defences: he will be my conceivings
Jah'zah, same as Jahazah
Jah'ze el, God will divide (apportion)
Jah'ze el ites, patronymic of preceding
Jah'ze rah, he will lead to the crown: he will be narrow-eyed
Jah'zi el, he will be divided of God
Ja'ir, he will stir up (1 Ch. 20: 5)
Ja'ir (2), he will enlighten
Ja'i rite, patronymic of Jair (2)
Ja i'rus, Greek for Jair (2)
Ja'kan, same as Jaakan
Ja'keh, he shall be cleared: he will be obedient: he will be pious
Ja'kim, he will set up
Ja'lon, he will abide
Jam'bres, foamy healer (?)
James, Greek form of Jacob
Ja'min, the right hand
Ja'min ites, patronymic of Jamin
Jam'lech, let him reign
Jan'na, he oppressed (?)
Jan'nes, he vexed: he oppressed
Ja no'ah, he will give rest
Ja no'hah, he will lead to rest
Ja'num, he will slumber
Ja'pheth, let him spread out
Ja phi'a, causing brightness
Japh'let, let him escape
Japh'le ti, patronymic of preceding
Ja'pho, to be fair to him
Ja'rah, honey-wood: honeycomb
Ja'reb, let him contend
Ja'red, a descender
Jar e si'ah, honey which is of Jah
Jar'ha, the month of sweeping away (?)
Ja'rib, he will contend

Jar'muth, he will be lifted up: elevation
Ja ro'ah, to lunate (*shine* as the *moon*)
Ja'shen, asleep
Ja'sher, righteous
Ja sho'be am, the people will return
Ja'shub, he will return
Jash' u bi le'hem, he will be restorer of bread (or of war)
Ja'shub ites, patronymic of Jashub
Ja'si el, same as Jaasiel
Ja'son, healer (?)
Jas'per, he will be made bare: he will be made prominent
Jath'ni el, he will be hired of God
Jat'tir, excellent: he will search out
Ja'van, the effervescing (one): mired
Ja'zer, same as Jaazer
Ja'ziz, he will cause to abound
Je'ar im, forests
Je at'e rai, my profits: my steps: my remainders
Je ber e chi'ah, whom Jehovah will bless
Je'bus, he will be trodden down
Jeb'u si, same as following
Jeb'u sites, gentilic of Jebus
Jec a mi'ah, Jah will establish: let Jah arise
Jech o li'ah, the prevailing of Jehovah
Jech o ni'as, Greek form of Jeconiah
Jec o li'ah, the prevailing of Jah
Jec o ni'ah, Jehovah will establish
Je da'iah, praise thou Jah (1 Ch. 4: 17; Neh. 3: 10)
Je da'iah (2), know thou Jah
Je di'a el, will be made known of God
Je di'dah, beloved
Jed i di'ah, beloved of Jah
Jed'u thun, let them give praise
Je e'zer, helpless: coast of help
Je e'zer ites, patronymic of preceding
Je'gar sa ha du'tha, heap of witness
Je ha le'le el, he will praise God
Je hal'e lel, same as preceding

Jeh dei'ah, he will be gladdened of Jehovah
Je hez'e kel, God shall strengthen
Je hi'ah, Jah shall save alive
Je hi'el, God shall save alive (2 Ch. 29: 14)
Je hi'el (2), swept away of God
Je hi'e li, patronymic of Jehiel (1)
Je hiz ki'ah, i.q. Hezekiah
Je ho'a dah, Jehovah is adornment
Je ho ad'dan, Jehovah their adornment
Je ho'a haz, Jehovah is taker-hold
Je ho'ash, Jehovah hath founded
Je ho'ha nan, Jehovah is gracious giver
Je hoi'a chin, Jehovah will establish
Je hoi'a da, Jehovah is knower
Je hoi'a kim, Jehovah will set up
Je hoi'a rib, Jehovah will contend
Je hon'a dab, Jehovah is willing giver
Je hon'a than, Jehovah is giver
Je ho'ram, Jehovah is exalted
Je ho shab'e ath, Jehovah's oath
Je hosh'a phat, Jehovah is judge
Je hosh'e ba, Jehovah is an oath
Je hosh'u a´,
Je hosh'u ah, } Jehovah is salvation
Je ho'vah, he is, he was (there are but two tenses in Hebrew, viz.,
    the past, and the future; the latter denoting what is con-
    tinued even in the present)
Je ho'vah ji'reh, Jehovah will see (provide)
Je ho'vah nis'si, Jehovah my banner
Je ho'vah roph'i, Jehovah healing
Je ho'vah sha'lom, Jehovah is peace
Je ho'vah sham'mah, Jehovah is there
Je ho'vah tsid ke'nu, Jehovah our righteousness
Je hoz'a bad, Jehovah is endower
Je hoz'a dak, Jehovah is the righteous (one)
Je'hu, he shall be (subsist)
Je hub'bah, he was hidden
Je hu'cal, Jehovah will prevail: he will be prevailed over

Je′hud, he will be praised

Je hu′di, patronymic of preceding (written also " Jew ")

Je hu di′jah, Jah will be praised (written also " Jewess ")

Je′hush, he will succor: he will assemble (or hasten)

Je i′el, swept away of God

Je kab′ze el, he will be gathered of God

Jek a me′am, let the people be established

Jek a mi′ah, let Jah arise: let Jah establish

Je ku′thi el, veneration of God: preservation of God

Je mi′ma, he will spoil (mar) her

Je mu′el, he will be made slumber of God

Jeph′thae, Greek form of Jephthah

Jeph′thah, he will open

Je phun′neh, he will be turned (prepared)

Je′rah, lunar

Je rah′me el, may God show mercy

Je rah′me el ites, patronymic of preceding

Je′red, same as Jared

Jer′e ma i, let me have promotions

Jer e mi′ah, Jah will cast forth

Jer e mi′as, Greek form of Jeremiah

Jer′e moth, let there be liftings up

Jer′e my, same as Jeromias

Je ri′ah, the fear of Jehovah: Jehovah will teach

Jer′i ba i, my contenders

Jer′i cho, let him smell it

Jer′i cho (2), place of fragrance: his fragrance (1. Kings 16: 34)

Je ri′el, may God teach

Je ri′jah, teach thou, Jah

Jer′i moth, there shall be elevations

Je′ri oth, curtains

Jer o bo′am, let the people contend: he will multiply the people

Je ro′ham, he shall find mercy

Je rub′ba al, Baal will be contended (with): Baal will be taught

Je rub′be sheth, let the shame (ful thing) contend

Je ru′el, fear ye God: taught of God

Je ru′sa lem, dual peace shall be taught: lay (set) ye double
    peace

Je ru'sha, possessed

Je ru'shah, possession

Je sa'iah, save thou, Jah

Je sha'iah, same as preceding

Je sha'iah, save thou, Jehovah (Ezr. 8: 7, 19)

Je sha'nah, old (as if withered)

Jesh ar'e lah, right towards God

Je sheb'e ab, father's dwelling

Je'sher, righteous

Jesh'i mon, the wilderness

Je shish' a i, my ancients

Je sho ha i'ah, he will be bowed down of Jah

Jesh'u a, }
Jesh'u ah, } he will save: Jehovah is salvation

Jesh'u run, the righteous one: a little righteous

Je si'ah, he will be lent of Jehovah

Je sim'i el, he will be placed of God

Jes'se, my men (1 Ch. 2: 13)

Jes'se (2), of him who is: my subsistences (?)

Jes'u i, same as Ishui, Ishuai, Isui

Jes'u ites, patronymic of preceding

Jes'u run, same as Jeshurun

Je'sus, Greek form of Jehoshua

Je'ther, a remnant: excellence

Je'theth, a tent pin: nail

Jeth'lah, he will hang

Je'thro, same as Jether, which is correct spelling (Ex. 4: 18)

Je'thro (2), his remnant: his excellence

Je'tur, he will arrange: he will encircle

Je'u el, same as Jeiel (*i.e.* swept away of God)

Je'ush, he will succor

Je'uz, he will take counsel

Jew, same as Jehudi

Jew'ess, Greek feminine of preceding

Jew'ish, Greek derivative of Jew

Jew'ry, same as Jehud

Jez a ni'ah, Jehovah will give ear: he will prostitute (*i.e.*, use illicitly the name of) Jehovah

Jez'e bel, non-cohabitant: unchaste

Je'zer, imagination: form: purpose

Je'zer ites, patronymic of preceding

Je zi'ah, he will be sprinkled of Jah

Je'zi el, let him be sprinkled of God

Jez li'ah, he shall pour out suitably; he will cause her to flow forth

Je zo'ar, whiteness, perhaps same as Zohar

Jez ra hi'ah, same as Izrahiah

Jez're el, it will be sown of God

Jez're el ite-s, patronymic of preceding

Jez're el i tess, feminine of preceding

Jib'sam, he will be fragrant

Jid'laph, he will weep (drop)

Jim'na
Jim'nah, } right-handed: he will number

Jim'nites, patronymic of preceding

Jiph'tah, he shall open

Jiph'thah el, God will open

Jo'ab, Jehovah is father

Jo'ah, Jehovah is brother

Jo'a haz, same as Jehoahaz

Jo an'na, Jehovah is gracious giver, Greek for Jehohanan

Jo'ash, Jehovah has become man

Jo'ash (2), Jehovah has helped (1 Ch. 7: 8–27: 28)

Jo'a tham, Greek for Jotham

Job, the cry of woe: I will exclaim

Job (2), he will cry (Gen. 46: 13)

Jo'bab, he will cause crying

Joch'e bed, Jehovah is glorious

Jo'ed, Jehovah is witness

Jo'el, Jehovah is God

Jo e'lah, let him be profitable: he will sweep away the strong

Jo e'zer, Jehovah is help

Jog'be hah, he will be elevated

Jog'li, he will carry me captive

Jo'ha, Jehovah is living: he will lead: lead thou, Jehovah

Jo ha'nan, Jehovah is gracious giver

John, Greek for preceding

Joi'a da, same as Jehoiada

Joi'a kim, Jehovah will establish

Joi'a rib, Jehovah will contend

Jok'de am, burning of the people: let the people kindle

Jo'kim, the arising of Jehovah

Jok'me am, he will establish the people

Jok'ne am, the people will be purchased: the people will be lamented

Jok'shan, their snare

Jok'tan, he will be made small

Jok'the el, absolved of God: or perhaps i.q. Jekuthiel

Jo'na, Greek for Jonah

Jon'a dab, Jehovah is willing giver

Jo'nah, a dove

Jo'nan, Greek for Johanan

Jo'nas, Greek for Jonah

Jo'nath e'lem re cho'kim, the dove of silence among strangers (literally the dove of silence of distances)

Jon'a than, Jehovah is giver

Jop'pa, fair to him (same as Japho)

Jo'rah, let him teach

Jo'ra i, my early rains: my teachers

Jo'ram, Jehovah has exalted

Jor'dan, their descent

Jo'rim, Greek for Joram

Jor ko'am, the people will be spread out: the people will be lean

Jos'a bad, Jehovah is bestower

Jos'a phat, Greek for Jehoshaphat

Jo'se, same as Joses

Jos'e dech, Jehovah is the righteous one

Jo'seph, let him add

Jo'seph (2), add thou Jehovah (Ps. 81: 5)

Jo'ses, Greek for Josiah

Jo'shah, he will be prospered: let him subsist: he will be made wise

Josh'a phat, Jehovah is judge

Josh a vi'ah, he will be prospered of Jah: may Jah sustain him

Josh bek'a shah, dwelling in hardness
Jo sheb bas'se bet, sitting in the seat (2 Sam. 23: 8, marg.)
Josh'u a, same as Jehoshua
Jo si'ah, he will be sustained of Jehovah
Jo si'as, Greek for preceding
Jos i bi'ah, Jah will make to dwell
Jos i phi'ah, Jah will add
Jot'bah, she was good
Jot'bath, } place of goodness
Jot'ba thah, }
Jo'tham, Jehovah is perfect
Joz'a bad, same as Josabad
Joz'a char, Jehovah is rememberer
Joz'a dak, Jehovah is the righteous (one)
Ju'bal, he will be carried
Ju'cal, he will be made able
Ju'da, Greek for Judah
Ju dæ'a, land of Judah
Ju'dah, he shall be praised
Ju'das, Greek for preceding
Ju'das is car'i ot, see Judas and Iscariot
Jude, same as Judas
Ju de'a, land of Judah
Ju'dith, Jewish: Jews' language
Ju'li a, feminine of following
Ju'li us, downy: hairy
Ju'ni a, youthful (if Latin): continue thou, Jah
Ju'pi ter, through (with the idea of *first cause*)
Ju shab'he sed, mercy shall be restored
Just'us, just
Jut'tah, he will be turned aside (or extended)

Kab'ze el, gathered of God
Ka'desh, apartness (*set apart* for purpose)
Ka'desh bar'ne a, the son of wandering was set apart
Kad'mi el before (literally in front of) God
Kad'mon ites, ancients: orientals
Kal'la i, my swiftnesses (or light ones)

Ka'nah, he has purchased
Ka re'ah, being bald
Ka'rem, a vineyard (?) (Josh. xv. 59, LXX)
Kar'ka a, to the bottom
Kar'kor, battering down
Kar'na im, double horn
Kar'tah, her hap: her meeting-place
Kar'tan, their hap: their meeting-place
Kat'tath, diminished
Ke'dar, darkness
Ked'e mah, eastward
Ked'e moth, beginnings: confrontings
Ke'desh, a sanctuary
Ke hel'a thah, convocation
Kei'lah, let the faint be alienated
Ke la'iah, lightly esteemed of Jah: voice of Jah
Kel'i ta, lacking: stunted
Ke mu'el, avenge ye God
Ke'nan, their smith (fabricator)
Ke'nath, possession
Ke'naz, the nest sprinkled (?)
Ken'ez ite-s, gentilic and patronymic of preceding
Ken'ite, a smith: a fabricator
Ken'ite (2), gentilic of preceding
Ken'iz zite, same as Kenezite
Ker'en hap'puch, the horn of paint
Ke'ri oth, cities
Ke'ros, stooping
Ke tu'rah, incense
Ke zi'a, cassia
Ke'ziz, cutting off
Kib'roth hat ta'a vah, the graves of lust
Kib za'im, double gathering: two heaps
Kid'ron, the mourner: the black one
Ki'nah, a lamentation
Kir, a wall
Kir har'a seth, an earthen wall
Kir har'e seth, same as preceding

Kir ha'resh, the wall is earthen
Kir he'res, the wall is earthen
Kir i a tha'im, double city
Kir'i oth, cities
Kir'jath, a (certain) city
Kir jath a'im, same as Kiriathaim
Kir jath ar'ba, city of four
Kir jath a'rim, city of enemies: city of cities
Kir jath ba'al, city of Baal
Kir jath hu'zoth, city of streets: city of broad ways
Kir jath je'ar im, city of forests
Kir jath san'nah, city of the thorn-bush
Kir jath se'pher, city of the book
Kish, a snare
Kish'i, my snare
Kish'i on, hardness
Ki'shon, ensnarer
Ki'shon (2), same as Kishion (Josh. 21: 28)
Ki'son, same as Kishon
Kith'lish, as if she would knead: wall of a man (?)
Kit'ron, incense-burner
Kit'tim, beaters down: crushers
Ko'a, alienation: a prince
Ko'hath, waiting: obedient: assembly
Ko'hath ites, patronymic of Kohath
Kol a i'ah, voice of Jah
Ko'rah, ice: bald
Ko'rah ites, patronymic of Korah
Ko'rath ites, same as preceding
Ko're, calling: happening: partridge
Ko're (sons of), same as Korahites
Kor'hites, same as preceding
Koz, a thorn
Kush a'iah, bow of Jehovah: snare of Jehovah
Ku'lon, comprehension (Josh. xv. 59, LXX)

La'a dah, for adornment
La'a dan, for their adornment

La′ban, white
La′chish, walk of a man
La′el, unto God
La′had, towards exultant shout
La ha′i ro i, unto the living (one) seeing me
Lah′mam, to the violent: their bread
Lah′mi, my bread
La′ish, to knead (reading of some copies in 2 Sam. 3: 15)
La′ish (2), a lion
La′kum, the rising up
La′ma, why?
La′mech, why thus with thee?: unto bringing low
La od i ce′a, the people's rights
La od i ce′ans, gentilic of preceding
Lap′i doth, torches: unto the calamities
La se′a, shaggy
La′sha, unto blindness (by *covering* the eyes)
La sha′ron, unto Sharon (see Sharon)
Lat′in, of Rome's strength
Laz′ar us, Greek for Eleazar
Le′ah, weary
Le an′noth, to affliction
Leb′a na
Leb′a nah, } whiteness: the moon
Leb′an on, whiteness
Leb′a oth, lionesses
Leb bæ′us, a laver (?)
Le bo′nah, frankincense (from its whitness)
Le′cah, go thou
Le′ha bim, flames: blades (as *glittering*)
Le′hi, cheek: jawbone
Lem′u el, unto God
Le′shem, unto desolation
Le tu′shim, sharpened ones: hammered ones
Le um′mim, peoples (as *massed* together)
Le′vi, joined
Le vi′a than, a coiled animal: their burrowing: their union
Le′vite, patronymic of Levi

Le vit′i cal, concerning Levi
Li′ber tines, freedmen
Lib′nah, whiteness
Lib′ni, my whiteness
Lib′nites, patronymic of preceding
Lib′y a, afflicted
Lib′y a (2), perhaps Greek for preceding or possibly " weeping "
Lib′y ans (1), empty-hearted (Dan. 11: 43)
Lib′y ans (2), gentilic of Libya, (1) (Jer. 46: 9)
Li′gure, same as Leshem
Lik′hi, my doctrine
Li′nus, linen
Lo am′mi, not my people
Lod, travail: to bear
Lo de′bar, not a word (*i.e.,* nothing)
Lo′is, no standard-bearer: no flight
Lord (in small caps.), Jehovah: occasionally " Jah "
Lord, master, rarely used as a divine title, save when in connec-
   tion with God
Lo ru ha′mah, not shown mercy
Lot, a wrapping
Lo′tan, their covering
Lu′bim-s, same as Libyans (2)
Lu′cas, a light: white
Lu′ci fer, howling: shining one
Lu′ci us, light: bright: white
Lud, to the firebrand: travailing
Lu′dim, to the firebrands: travailings
Lu′hith, tabular: pertaining to the table
Luke, same as Lucas
Luz, perverse
Lyc a o′ni a, wolfish (?)
Ly′ci a, wolfish
Lyd′da, travail
Lyd′i a, to firebrand: travailing
Lyd′i ans, plural of preceding
Ly sa′ni as, relaxing sadness
Ly′si as, releaser
Lys′tra, ransoming

Ma'a cah,
Ma'a chah, } pressure (literally she has pressed)'

Ma ach'a thi,
Ma ach'a thites, } patronymic of preceding

Ma ad'ai, my unclothings: my slidings: my adornings

Ma a di'ah, adorned of Jah: shaken of Jah

Ma a'i, my bowels

Ma al'eh ac rab'bim, ascent of the scorpions

Ma'ar ath, naked place

Ma a se'iah, work of Jehovah

Ma a se'iah (2), Jah is a refuge (Jer. 32: 12–51: 59)

Ma as'i ai, my works

Ma'ath, from this time

Ma'az, counsellor: shutting

Ma a zi'ah, strengthened of Jehovah

Mac e do'ni a, tall (?)

Mac e do'ni an, derivative of preceding

Mach'ba nai, he brought low my sons

Mach'be nah, he brought low the building

Ma'chi, my poverty

Ma'chir, a salesman

Ma'chir ites, a patronymic of preceding

Mach na de'bai, he brought low my willing ones

Mach pe'lah, doubling: he brought low the set apart

Mad'a i, my measures: my garments: what is enough

Ma'di an, Greek for Midian

Mad man'nah, dung-heap: thou art simulating a garment

Mad'men, dung-hill: garment of simulation

Mad me'nah, same as preceding with feminine termination

Ma'don, strife

Mag'bish, crystallizing

Mag'da la, a tower

Mag da le'ne, gentilic of preceding

Mag'di el, my preciousness is God

Ma'gog, overtopping: covering

Ma gor mis'sa bib, fear from around about

Mag'pi ash, plague of the moth: the plague is consumed

Ma'ha lah, sickness

Ma ha la'le el, praise of God

Ma'ha lath, making sick: sickness: appeasing

Ma'ha lath le an'noth, preceding with Leannoth

Ma'ha li, my sickness

Ma ha na'im, double camp

Ma'ha neh dan', the camp of Dan

Ma har'a i, my hastenings

Ma'hath, snatching

Ma'hav ite, declarers: propagators: assemblers: living ones

Ma ha'zi oth, visions

Ma'her shal'al hash'baz, quickly the spoil, hasting the prey

Mah'lah, sickness

Mah'li, my sickness

Mah'lites, patronymic of preceding

Mah'lon, sickness

Ma'hol, a dance

Ma'kaz, cutting off

Mak'he loth, congregations

Mak ke'dah, branding (spotting) place

Mak'tesh, a mortar (braying place)

Mal'a chi, my messenger

Mal'cham, their king

Mal chi'ah, my king is Jehovah

Mal'chi el, my king is God

Mal'chi el ites, patronymic of preceding

Mal chi'jah, my king is Jehovah

Mal chi'ram, my king is exalted

Mal chi shu'a, my king is salvation: king of opulence

Mal'chus, kingly

Ma le'le el, same as Mahalaleel

Mal'lo thi, I have spoken

Mal'luch, kingly

Mam'mon, wealth (as *trusted* in)

Mam're, causing fatness

Man'a en, Greek for Menahem,

Man'a hath, resting-place

Ma na'heth ites, feminine plural of gentilic of preceding (1 Ch.
2: 52)

Ma na'heth ites, patronymic of Manahath

Ma nas'seh, causing to forget

Ma nas'ses, Greek for preceding

Ma nas'sites, patronymic of Manasseh

Ma'neh, a weight: (as a standard, from *Manah* = "to number"

Ma no'ah, rest

Ma no'cho, his rest (Josh. xv. 59, LXX)

Ma'och, pressing: squeezing

Ma'on, habitation

Ma'on ites, gentilic of preceding

Ma'ra, he was arrogant: bitterness

Ma'rah, he rebelled: bitterness

Mar'a lah, causing shaking

Mar a nath'a, the Lord comes

Mar'cus, a defence (?)

Ma re'shah, headship: forget to be arrogant

Mark, English form of Marcus

Ma'roth, bitternesses

Mar'se na, bitter is the thorn-bush

Mars hill, same as Areopagus

Mar'tha, she was rebellious

Ma'ry, Greek for Miriam

Mas'chil, giving understanding

Mash, he departed: he felt (groped)

Ma'shal, a parable: a parabolist

Mas're kah, place of the choice vine

Mas'sa, a prophecy: a burden (as something *undertaken* to carry through); enduring

Mas'sah, temptation: she fainted

Ma thu'sa la, Greek for Methuselah

Ma'tred, causing pursuit: continuing

Ma'tri, he of the rain: rainy

Mat'tan, a gift

Mat'tan ah, a gift: givingness

Mat ta ni'ah, gift of Jehovah

Mat'ta tha, Greek for following

Mat'ta thah, givingness

Mat ta thi'as, Greek for Mattithiah

Mat te na′i, my gifts

Mat′than, Greek for Mattan

Mat′that, abbreviated form of Matthias

Mat′thew, an abbreviated form of Mattathias

Mat thi′as, another form of preceding

Mat ti thi′ah, gift of Jehovah

Maz′zar oth, scatterings (?)

Me′ah, an hundred

Me a′rah, a cave (from to *strip, lay bare*)

Me bun′nai, my buildings

Mech′e rath ite, he of the dug-out: he of the digging tool

Me′dad, would be loving

Me′dan, strife: discernment

Mede, my measure: my garment

Med′e ba, waters of rest (quiet)

Medes, he of the measured: my garments

Me′di a, same as preceding

Me′di an, Chaldee, emphatic of Madai

Me gid′do, invading: gathering for cutting (self): his cutting-place

Me gid′don, the cutter: brander

Me het′a beel, God's best

Me het′a bel, same as preceding

Me hi′da, allegorist

Me′hir, a price

Me ho′lah, see Abel-meholah

Me hol′ath ite, gentilic of preceding

Me hu′ja el (1), blot ye out that Jah is God (Gen. 4: 18)

Me hu′ja el (2), blot thou out that my Jah is God (2d name)

Me hu′man, their discomfiture

Me hu′nim-s, habitations

Me jar′kon, waters of mildew: waters of verdure

Me ko′nah, a settlement (or *base*)

Mel a ti′ah, Jah's (way of) escape

Mel′chi, Greek for Melchiah

Mel chi′ah, another form of Malchiah

Mel chis′e dec, Greek for Melchizedek

Mel chi shu′a, same as Malchishua

Mel chiz′e dek, king of righteousness

Me′le a, my dear friend: object of care

Me′lech, a king

Mel′i cu, my royalty: they have made a king

Mel′i ta, of honey: escaping

Mel′zar, the circumcised, he straitened

Mem′phis, being made fair: but if Greek, " blamable " " encompassed "

Me mu′can, their poverty

Men′a hem, comforter

Me′nan, soothsayer: enchanted

Me′ne, he has numbered

Me′on, see Baal-meon

Me on′e nim, observers of times

Me on′o thai, my dwellings

Meph′a ath, the shining forth

Me phib′o sheth, breathing shame

Me′rab, increasing

Mer a i′ah, rebellion: provoking Jah

Me ra′ioth, rebellions

Me ra′ri, my bitterness

Me ra′rites, patronymic of preceding

Mer a tha′im, double rebellion: double bitterness

Mer cu′ri us, eloquent: learned: shrewd: crafty

Me′red, rebellion

Mer′e moth, elevations

Me′res, moisture: fracture

Mer′i bah, strife

Mer′i bah Ka′desh, strife of Kadesh (see Kadesh)

Me rib′ba al, Baal is contentious

Me rib′ba al (2), rebellion of Baal (1 Ch. 9: 40, 2d name)

Me ro′dach, thy rebellion

Me ro′dach bal′a dan, Merodach is not a lord: thy rebellion, Baal is lord

Me′rom, the lifting up

Me ron′o thite, the joyful shouter

Me′roz, waxing lean: enduring: cedar worker

Me′sech, a drawing: a purchase (as mechanical advantage)

Me'sha (1), bringing deliverance

Me'sha, (2) waters of devastation: making to forget: equalizing: existing (1 Ch. 8: 9 — Gen. 10: 30)

Me'shach, waters of quiet: who is what thou art?: biting

Me'shech, a drawing same as Mesech

Me shel e mi'ah, Jah is reconciliation: bringing peace-offering of Jah

Me she za' beel, delivered of God

Me shil'le mith, reconciliation

Me shil'le moth, reconciliations

Me sho'bab, restored: backsliding

Me shul'lam, reconciled: recompensed

Me shul'le meth, reconciliation

Me so'ba ite, the one set up of Jah

Mes o po ta'mi a, exalted

Mes si'ah, the anointed

Mes si'as, Greek for preceding

Me theg am'mah, the bridle of a cubit

Me thu'sa el, they died enquiring: they died who are of God: man who is of God

Me thu'se lah, they died — the dart: man of the dart

Me u'nim, same as Mehunim

Mez'a hab, waters of gold

Mi'a min, from the right hand

Mib'har, choicest

Mib'sam, fragrant

Mib'zar, a fortress

Mi'cah, who is like Jehovah?

Mi ca'iah, who is as Jehovah?

Mi'cha, who is like Jehovah?

Mi'cha el, who is as God?

Mi'chah, same as Micah

Mi cha'iah, who is like Jehovah?

Mi'chal, a brook: or possibly contraction of Michael

Mich'mas, treasury: poverty was melted: poverty of servile work

Mich'mash, poverty was felt: poverty has departed

Mich'me thah, the poverty of the dead: the poverty of the reward

Mich'ri, my price

Mich'tam, the poverty of the perfect: (blood) staining (*i.e.*, deep dyeing)

Mid'din, from judgment: judging

Mid'i an, contention: strife

Mid'i an ites, gentilic of preceding

Mid'i an i tish, pertaining to Midian

Mig'da lel, tower of God

Mig'dal gad, tower of Gad

Mig'dol, a tower

Mig'ron, hurling down

Mij'a min, from the right hand

Mik'loth, sprouts: triflings

Mik ne'iah, acquisition of Jehovah

Mil a la'i, my utterances

Mil'cah, a queen

Mil'com, reigning

Mi le'tum, cared for

Mi le'tus, cared for

Mil'lo, a fill (earthwork)

Mi ni'a min, from the right hand

Min'ni, from me

Min'nith, apportionment (or literally " from-me-dom ")

Miph'kad, muster: apportionment

Mir'i am, their rebellion

Mir'ma, deceit

Mis'gab, a high place

Mish'a el, who is what God is?

Mi'shal, enquiry

Mi'sham, their regarding: their cleansing

Mi'she al, same as Mishal

Mish'ma, a hearing: (*i.e.*, a report — what is heard)

Mish man'nah, fattening

Mish'pat, judgment

Mish'ra ites, touching evil (as removing, or drawing out)

Mis pe'reth, enumerator

Mis're photh ma'im, burnings of waters

Mith'cah, sweetness

Mith'nite, an athlete (literally, he of loins): a giver

Mith're dath, remainder of law: searching out of law

Mi ty le'ne, curtailed (?)

Mi'zar, little

Miz'pah, watch-tower

Miz'par, a number

Miz'peh, a watch-tower

Miz ra'im, double straitness

Miz'zah, from sprinkling

Mna'son (Na'son), solicitor: the number is safe

Mo'ab, from father: what father?

Mo'ab ites, patronymic and gentilic of Moab

Mo'ab i tess, feminine of preceding

Mo'ab i tish, pertaining to Moab

Mo a di'ah, the set time of Jah

Mo la'dah, birth: bringing forth

Mo'lech, the king (it always has the article, and is vocalized the same as "bosheth," which some think is to denote "shame")

Mo'lid, causing to bring forth

Mo'loch, a king

Mo'ras thite, gentilic of Moresheth Gath

Mor'de cai, bitterness of my oppressed

Mor'reh, teacher: former rain

Mor'esh eth gath, possession of Gath

Mo ri'ah, my teacher is Jah: seen of Jah

Mo se'ra, bondage

Mo se'roth, bonds

Mo'ses, drawing out

Mo'za, a going forth

Mo'zah, wringing out

Mup'pim, shakings: wavings

Mu'shi, my yielding: my departure: depart thou

Mu'shites, patronymic of preceding

Muth lab'ben, the death of the son

My'ra, myrrh: myrtle juice

My'sia, closure: abomination

Na'am, pleasant
Na'am ah, pleasantness
Na'am an, pleasantness
Na'a ma thite, gentilic of Naamah
Na'am ites, patronymic of Naaman
Na'a rah, a maiden
Na'a rai, my boys: my shakings: my roarings
Na'a ran, their boy: (or maiden)
Na'a rath, to maidenhood: maiden-place
Na ash'on, a diviner
Na as'son, Greek for preceding
Na'bal, foolish
Na'both, increasings
Na'chon, established
Na'chor, snorter
Na'dab, the willing one
Nag'ge, my shinings
Na'ha lal, tended (as in a pasture)
Na ha'li el, valley (or river) of God
Na hal'lal, more properly "Nahalal"
Na'ha lol, being tended — see Nahalal
Na'ham, comforter
Na ham'a ni, he comforted me
Na har'a i, my snortings
Na'ha ri, same as preceding
Na'hash, a serpent
Na'hath, rest: descent
Nah'bi, my hiding
Na'hor, same as Nachor
Nah'shon, a diviner
Na'hum, comforted
Na'in, afflicted: beautiful
Na'ioth, abodes
Na'o mi, my pleasantness
Na'phish, refreshing
Naph'ta li, my wrestling: my tortuoscity
Naph'tu him, openings
Nar cis'sus, narcotic

Na′than, a giver

Na than′a el, given of God

Na′than me′lech, the king's gift

Na′um, Greek for Nahum

Naz a rene′, gentilic of following

Naz′a reth, a branch: preservation

Naz′a rites, separated

Ne′ah, a wandering: a shaking

Ne ap′o lis, new city

Ne a ri′ah, shaken of Jah: child of Jah

Neb′a i, my fruits

Ne ba′ioth, prophecies: increasings: heights

Ne ba′joth, prophetesses

Ne bal′lat, secret folly

Ne′bat, beheld: we shall speak idly

Ne′bo, his prophecy

Neb u chad nez′zar, confusing the lord of treasure: prophesy, the earthen vessel is preserved

Neb u chad rez′zar, confusion of the abode of treasure: prophesy, the seer's vessel is preserved

Neb u shas′ban, prophesy their deliverance

Neb u zar′a dan, prophesy, the lord is estranged

Ne′cho, his smiting

Ned a bi′ah, givingness of Jah

Neg′i nah, a harp-song

Neg′i noth, harp-songs

Ne′go, see Abednego

Ne hel′am ite, he of the dream

Ne he mi′ah, comfort of Jah

Ne′hil oth, we shall cause profanation: we shall divide the in- heritance

Ne′hum, comfort

Ne hush′ta, bronzed

Ne hush′tan, a bit of bronze

Ne′i el, we shall be shaken of God

Ne′keb, a varying (groove?)

Ne ko′da, spotted

Ne mu′el, they (were made to) slumber of God

Ne mu'el ites, patronymic of preceding
Ne'pheg, we shall cease (grow numb)
Ne'phish, refreshing
Ne phish'e sim, we shall shake the spoilers: refreshed of spices
Neph'tha lim, Greek for Naphtali
Neph to'ah, opening
Ne phu'sim, scatter spices: expansions
Ner, a lamp
Ne're us, a water nymph (ancient sea-god)
Ner'gal, the lamp rolled
Ner'gal shar e'zer, the rolling lamp observed the treasure
Ne'ri, Greek for Neriah
Ne ri'ah, my lamp is Jehovah
Ne than'e el, given of God
Neth a ni'ah, given of Jehovah
Neth'i nim-s, given ones
Ne to'phah, dropping: distillation
Ne toph'a thi, gentilic of preceding
Ne toph'a thite, same as preceding
Ne zi'ah, we shall oversee
Ne'zib, a garrison
Nib'haz, we shall utter (what is) seen
Nib'shan, we shall prophesy quiet: smoothed (?)
Ni ca'nor, untimely victory
Nic o de'mus, conqueror of the populace
Nic o la'i tans, conqueror of (what is of) the people
Nic'o las, conqueror of the people (as a whole)
Ni cop'o lis, conquest of the city
Ni'ger, black (probably Latin)
Nim'rah, he was rebellious: leopardess
Nim'rim, rebellious ones: leopards
Nim'rod, we will rebel
Nim'shi, my being drawn
Nin'e ve, Greek for Nineveh
Nin'e veh, offspring of ease: offspring abiding
Nin'e vites, gentilic of preceding
Ni'san, their flight
Nis'roch, ensign of delicateness

No, disrupting, frustrating
No a di'ah, convened of Jah: meeting of Jah
No'ah, rest
No'ah (2), movable (name of female)
No a'mon, see No and Amon
Nob, fruit: empty: or possibly same as Nebo
No'bah, a barking
Nod, wandering
No'dab, liberal
No'e, Greek for Noah (1)
No'gah, brightness
No'hah, quietude
Non, same as Nun
Noph, presentability
No'phah, breathing: blowing
Nun, perpetuity
Nym'phas, bridal

O ba di'ah, serving Jehovah
O'bal, heaping confusion
O'bed, serving
O'bed e'dom, serving Edom
O'bil, causing mourning
O'both, necromancers: water skins
Oc'ran, their trouble
O'ded, restoration: surrounding
Og, hearth-cake
O'had, he shouted
O'hel, a tent
Ol'i vet, olive yard
O lym'pas, celestial (?): (in mythology — the god of games)
O'mar, I will say
O'me ga, finality: *last* letter of Greek alphabet
Om'ri, my sheaf (as *bound*)
On, vigor: strength: iniquity
O'nam, their vigor (masculine): their iniquity
O'nan, their vigor (feminine): their iniquity
O nes'i mus, profitable

O ne siph′or us, profit-bringing
O′no, his vigor: his iniquity
O ny′cha, whose travail: roaring (as a lion)
O′nyx, setting them equal: justifying them
O′phel, swelling: tumor: mound
O′phir, reducing to ashes
Oph′ni, my flying: my darkness (?)
Oph′rah, dustiness: fawn-like (from its *color*)
O′reb, a raven·
O′ren, an ash: a fir: a cedar
O ri′on, a fool
Or′nan, light was perpetuated: their fir tree
Or′pah, her neck: neck-iness (?)
O′see, Greek for Hosea
O′she a, to save
Oth′ni, my seasonable speaking
Oth′ni el, seasonable speaking of God
O′zem, I shall hasten them
O zi′as, Greek for Uzziah
Oz′ni, my hearing: my ear
Oz′nites, patronymic of preceding

Pa a′ne ah, see Zaphnath-paaneah
Pa′a rai, my openings
Pa′dan, their ransom
Pa′dan a′ram, their ransom is high
Pa′don, ransom
Pa′gi el, event of God
Pa′hath mo′ab, pit of Moab
Pa′i, my groaning
Pa′lal, mediator: judge (as *intervening*)
Pal es ti′na, wallowing
Pal′es tine, another spelling of preceding
Pal′lu, wonderful
Pal′lu ites, patronymic of preceding
Pal′ti, my escape
Pal′ti el, deliverance of God
Pal′tite, same as Palti

Pam phyl'i a, all sorts: all tribes
Pan'nag, preparing of affliction
Pa'phos, suffering
Pa'rah, he increased: heifer
Pa'ran, their beautifying
Par'bar, he annulled the corn
Pa'rez, see Rimmon-parez
Par mash'ta, spoiled is the banquet
Par'me nas, one who abides
Par'nach, the bullock we smote
Pa'rosh, a flea
Par shan'da tha, he repeatedly broke the decree
Par'thi ans, a pledge (?)
Par'u ah, he was budded
Par va'im, he broke their hooks (?)
Pa'sach, thy vanishing: thy spreading out
Pas dam'mim, vanishing of bloods: he spread out bloods
Pa se'ah, vacillating: halting
Pash'ur, increasing of white (linen)
Pat'a ra, suffering it seems (?): scattering cursing
Path'ros, a morsel moistened
Path ru'sim, gentilic of preceding
Pat'mos, my killing
Pat'ro bas, father's walk
Pa'u, they cried
Paul, little
Paul'us, another form of preceding
Paz'zez, see Beth-pazzez
Ped'a hel, redeemed of God
Pe dah'zur, the rock has redeemed
Pe da'iah, redeemed of Jehovah
Pe'kah, opening
Pek a hi'ah, opening of Jah
Pe'kod, to visit
Pel a i'ah, distinguished of Jah
Pel a li'ah, intervention of Jah
Pel a ti'ah, Jehovah's (way of) escape
Pe'leg, a channel (as a *cleft, dividing*)

Pe′let, escape
Pe′leth, separation
Pe′leth ites, gentilic of preceding
Pel′o nite, a certain (unnamed) one
Pe ni′el, the face of God (literally, turn thou, God)
Pe nin′nah, a ruby
Pen′te cost, fiftieth
Pe nu′el, turn ye (to) God: the face of God
Pe′or, the opening
Per′a zim, breaches
Pe′res, has been (or *is*) divided
Pe′resh, dung
Pe′rez, breach
Pe′rez uz′za
Pe′rez uz′zah, } the breach was strengthened
Per′ga, much earth: very earthy
Per′ga mos, much marriage
Pe ri′da, separation
Per′iz zites, rustic: squatter (?)
Per′sia, he divided
Per′si an, gentilic of preceding
Per′sis, a Persian woman
Pe ru′da, separation: seed (as *separated*)
Pe′ter, a stone
Peth a hi′ah, opened of Jah
Pe′thor, to interpret
Pe thu′el, be ye persuaded of God: be ye enlarged of God
Pe ul′thai, my works: my wages
Pha′gor, to faint (Josh. xv. 59, lxx.)
Pha′lec, Greek for Peleg
Phal′lu, wonderful
Phal′ti, my escape
Phal′ti el, same as Paltiel
Pha nu′el, face of God: turn ye to God
Pha′raoh (fa′ro), his nakedness
Pha′raoh hoph′ra, his nakedness, covering evil
Pha′raoh ne′cho,
Pha′raoh ne′choh, } his nakedness, he is smitten

Pha'res, Greek for following
Pha'rez, a breach
Phar'i sees, the separated: expounders
Pha'rosh, same as Parosh
Phar'par, breaking asunder
Phar'zites, patronymic of Pharez
Pha se'ah, same as Paseah
Phe'be, radiant
Phe'let, see Beth-phelet
Phe ni'ce, palm-land (Acts 27: 12)
Phe ni'ce, palm: palm-tree
Phe ni'ci a, same as Phenice (1)
Phi'chol, mouth of all
Phil a del'phi a, brotherly love
Phi le'mon, one who kisses
Phi le'tus, beloved
Phil'ip, lover of horses (*i.e.*, the *race*)
Phi lip'pi, same as preceding
Phi lip'pi ans, gentilic of preceding
Phi lis'ti a, wallowing
Phi lis'tim, gentilic of preceding
Phi lis'tine-s, same as preceding
Phi lol'o gus, lover of the word
Phin'e has, mouth of pity
Phle'gon, burning
Phoe'be, same as Phebe
Phoe'nice, same as Phenice
Phoe ni'cia, same as Phenicia
Phryg'ia, parched (used for " female roaster ")
Phu'rah, he was fruitful
Phut, same as Libya, and Put
Phu'vah, he was scattered (as by a *puff*, a *blow*)
Phy gel'lus, a little fugitive
Pi be'seth, mouth of loathing
Pi ha hi'roth, the mouth of wrath kindlings: the mouth of caves
Pi'late, close pressed (as a piece of felt)
Pil'dash, he threshed the separated: iron (bolt?) of fire
Pil'e ha, cleavage

Pil e′ser, see Tiglath, and Tilgath
Pil ne′ser, see Tilgath-pilneser
Pil′tai, my escapes
Pi′non, distraction
Pi′ram, their wild ass
Pir′a thon, nakedness: looseness
Pir′a thon ite, gentilic of preceding
Pis′gah, survey
Pi sid′ia, persuasion of right
Pi′son, increase
Pis′pah, disappearance
Pi′thom, mouth of integrity
Pi′thon, mouth of a monster
Ple′ia des,′ for what?
Poch′e reth, here the cutting off
Pol′lux, Jupiter's young men
Pon′ti us, of the sea
Pon′tus, the sea
Por′a tha, fruitfulness: frustration
Por′ci us, swinish
Por′ci us fes′tus, swinish festival
Pot′i phar, my affliction was broken
Po tiph′e rah, affliction of the locks (of hair)
Præ to′ri um, the chief magistrate's court
Pris′ca, ancient
Pris cil′la, little old woman (diminutive of preceding)
Proch′o rus, leader of the dance: leader of praise
Ptol e ma′is (tol), warlike (?)
Pu′a, same as Phuvah
Pu′ah, he was scattered
Pu′ah (2), pained (as a woman in *travail*): displayed (Ex. 1 : 15)
Pub′li us, popular
Pu′dens, modest
Pu′hites, openness: simplicity: (ingenuous?)
Pul, distinguishing: separator (?)
Pu′nites, distracted: or gentilic of Phuvah
Pu′non, distraction
Pur, frustration: lot

Pu'rim, masculine plural of preceding
Put, afflicted
Pu te'o li, little (mineral) springs: chief justice (if Greek)
Pu'ti el, afflicted of God

Quar'tus, fourth (from Latin: as Greek it might be " and not a loaf ")

Ra'a mah, thunder
Ra a mi'ah, thunder of Jah
Ra am'ses, thunder of the standard
Rab'bah, populous
Rab'bath, populous
Rab'bi, my master
Rab'bith, multiplicity
Rab bo'ni, my chief master
Rab'mag, chief soothsayer: much melting
Rab'sa ris, chief eunuch
Rab'sha keh, chief cup-bearer
Ra'ca, vain: empty
Ra'chab, Greek for Rahab (2), *i.e.*, breadth
Ra'chal, trafficker
Ra'chel, a ewe
Rad'da i, my subduings
Ra'gau, Greek for Reu
Ra gu'el, associate with God (or literally " tend ye God ")
Ra'hab, arrogance
Ra'hab (2), breadth (the harlot, of Jericho)
Ra'ham, compassionate
Ra'hel, ewe: same as Rachel
Ra'kem, embroidery
Rak'kath, leanness: her spitting
Rak'kon, emaciation: spitting out
Ram, high
Ra'ma, } the height
Ra'mah, }
Ra'math, the height
Ra math a'im zoph'im, the double height of the watchers

Ra'math ite, patronymic of Ramah
Ra'math le'hi, jaw-bone height
Ra'math miz'peh, the watch-tower height
Ra me'ses, evil is the standard-bearer: or same as Raamses
Ra mi'ah, Jah has exalted: loosed of Jah
Ra'moth, heights: coral
Ra'moth gil'e ad, see Ramoth and Gilead
Ra'pha, he healed: the giant: the shrunken (in 1 Ch. 8: 2-20: 4, 6, 8)
Ra'pha (2), the giant: the feeble (one)
Ra'phu, healed
Re a i'a,
Re a i'ah, } seen of Jah
Re'ba, a fourth part
Re bec'ca, Greek for following
Re bek'ah, tying
Re'chab, charioteer: rider
Re'chab ites, gentilic of preceding
Re'chah, tenderness
Red sea, to come to an end: a reed (Amos 3: 15)
Red sea (2), a whirlwind (Job 37: 9)
Re el a'iah, shaken of Jah
Re'gem, stoning
Re gem'me lech, stoning of the king
Re ha bi'ah, enlarged of Jehovah
Re'hob, broad place (as modern " square, plaza ")
Re ho bo'am, enlargement of the people
Re ho'both, broad places
Re'hum, compassionate
Re'i, my friend
Re'kem, embroidery: variegation
Rem a li'ah, lifted up to Jehovah: bedecked of Jehovah
Re'meth, elevation
Rem'mon, pomegranate
Rem'mon meth o'ar, the marked-out pomegranate
Rem'phan, the shrunken (as lifeless)
Re'pha el, healed of God
Re'phah, enfeebling of the breath: healing of the breath

Reph a i'ah, healed of Jah: enfeebled of Jah
Reph'a im-s, the dead: giants: healers
Reph'i dim, supports: shrinking of hands
Re'sen, a bridle
Re'sheph, a flame
Re'u, associate ye: feed ye
Reu'ben, see ye, a son
Reu'ben ites, patronymic of preceding
Re u'el, associate ye with God: tend ye God
Re u'mah, raised up; see ye aught?
Re'zeph, burning: glowing
Re zi'a, haste: delight
Re'zin, delightsomeness
Re'zon, to wax lean: a prince
Rhe'gi um, a passage (as *broken through*)
Rhe'sa, Greek for Rephaiah
Rho'da, a rose
Rhodes, rosy
Ri'bai, my strengths
Rib'lah, the strife ended: fruitful
Rim'mon, pomegranate
Rim'mon (2), his pomegranate (1 Ch. 6: 77)
Rim'mon pa'rez, pomegranate of the breach
Rin'nah, a joyful shout
Ri'phath, bruising: shrivelling: healing
Ri'phath (2), slander: fault (Gen. 10: 3)
Ris'sah, moistening
Rith'mah, binding: broom-copse
Riz'pah, pavement: glowing
Ro bo'am, Greek for Rehoboam
Ro dan'im, breakers loose (see Do da'nim)
Ro ge'lim, footmen: treaders: fullers (?)
Roh'gah, fear cured: agitation
Ro mam ti e'zer, I have exalted the helper
Ro'man-s, strong
Rome, strength
Rosh, head: chief
Ru'fus, red (or if Greek, " supping up ")

Ru ha'mah, see Lo-ruhamah
Ru'mah, exaltation
Ruth, satisfied

Sa bach'tha ni, hast thou forsaken me?
Sab'a oth, hosts
Sa be'ans, drunkards
Sa be'ans (2), they who come: go about (busybodies?) (Joel 3: 8)
Sa be'ans (3), he who is coming (Job 1: 15)
Sab'ta, he compassed the chamber
Sab'tah, same as preceding: he compassed the mark
Sab'te cha, ⎱ he compassed the seat: he compassed the smit-
Sab'te chah, ⎰   ing
Sa'car, a hireling: wages
Sad'du cees, the righteous
Sa'doc, Greek for Zadok
Sa'la, Greek for following
Sa'lah, a missile (as *sent* forth)
Sal'a mis, a surging
Sa la'thi el, I have asked of God
Sal'cah, ⎱ he lifted up the blind: straitened basket
Sal'chah, ⎰
Sa'lem, at peace: complete: perfect
Sa'lim, tossing
Sal'la i, my baskets: my castings up
Sal'lu, they have raised up
Sal'ma, raiment
Sal'mon, image: resemblance (Ps. 68: 14)
Sal'mon (2), raiment: a garment (Ruth 4: 20)
Sal'mon (3), clothing
Sal mo' ne, from the surging
Sa lo'me, peaceable
Sa'lu, weighed
Sa ma'ri a, guardianship
Sa mar'i tan-s, of Samaria
Sam'gar ne'bo, spice dragged away is his prophecy (?)
Sam'lah, enwrapping

Sa'mos, a token: a sandy bluff
Sam o thra'ci a, Samos of Thrace: a sign of rags
Sam'son, little sun (?)
Sam'u el, his name (is) of God (?)
San bal'lat, hatred (or thorn) in secret
San'nah, see Kirjath-sannah
San san'nah, thorniness
Saph, a basin: a threshold
Saph'ir, fair
Sap phi'ra (saf fi'ra), a sapphire
Sap'phire, telling out: recounting
Sa'ra, ⎤
Sa'rah, ⎦ a princess
Sa'rah (2), the prince breathed (Num. 26: 46)
Sa'rai, my princesses
Sa'raph, a burner: fiery: fiery serpent
Sar'dine, a footstep
Sar'dis, red ones (?)
Sar'dites, patronymic of Sered
Sar'di us, ruddiness
Sar'do nyx, ruddy: (finger) nail colored (?)
Sa rep'ta, smelting: she hath refined
Sar'gon, stubborn rebel
Sa'rid, survivor: remainder
Sa'ron, rightness
Sar se'chim, prince of the coverts
Sa'ruch, Greek for Serug
Sa'tan, an adversary
Sa'tyr, a demon (in *he-goat* form, or as *bristling* with horror)
Saul, requested
Sce'va (se'va), mind reader
Scyth'i an, rude: rough
Sea, see Red Sea
Se'ba, drink thou
Se'bat, smite thou
Se ca'cah, enclosure
Se'chu, they hedged up
Se cun'dus, second

Se'gub, exalted (inaccessibly)
Se'ir, shaggy: hairy: goat-like
Se'i rath, the hairy she-goat
Se'la, } a rock: crag (2 Kings 14: 7)
Se'lah, }
Se'lah (2), make prominent
Se'la ham'mah le'koth, the rock of divisions
Se'led, recoil (?)
Sel eu ci'a, white light
Sem, Greek for Shem
Sem a chi'ah, sustained of Jehovah
Sem'e i, Greek form of Shemaiah
Sen'a ah, hatred (?)
Se'neh, thorny
Se'nir, bear the lamp (?)
Sen nach'e rib, the thorn laid waste
Sen'u ah, the hatred (?)
Se o'rim, barley: bearded ones
Se'phar, enumeration: census
Seph'a rad, end of wandering: end of spreading out
Seph ar va'im, enumeration, and twofold
Seph ar va'im (2), census of the sea (2 Kings 17: 31)
Se'phar vites, gentilic of Sepharvaim (1)
Se'rah, same as Sarah — the prince breathed
Ser a i'ah, prevailing of Jehovah: prince of Jehovah
Ser'aph ims, burners
Se'red, fright (?): stubbornness subdued
Ser'gi us, earth-born: born a wonder
Se'rug, intertwined
Seth, appointed: set
Se'thur, hidden
Sha al ab'bin, hand of skill: jackal of discernment
Sha al'bim, he regarded the hearts: he regarded the lions
Sha al'bo nite, gentilic of preceding
Sha'aph, who flew
Sha a ra'im, double gate
Sha ash'gaz, who succored the cut off
Shab beth'a i, my sabbaths

Shach'i a, the return of Jah: taken captive of Jah

Shad'da i, almighty

Sha'drach, the breast was tender

Sha'ge, erring

Sha'har, dawn: morning

Sha ha ra'im, double-dawn

Sha haz'i mah, to the proud ones: place of the proud

Sha'keh, see Rab-shakeh

Sha'lem, at peace: complete: safe: perfect

Sha'lim, handfuls

Shal'i sha, third (place)

Shal'le cheth, casting forth

Shal'lum, requital: restitution

Shal'lun, they spoiled them: he spoiled the lodging

Shal'mai, my garments: my peace-offerings

Shal'ma i (2) (a various reading, but probably meaning same as preceding)

Shal'man, he spoiled them: their peace-offering

Shal ma ne'ser, he spoiled them of the bond: their peace-offering of bondage

Sha'ma, a hearkener

Sham a ri'ah, guarded of Jah

Sha'med, guardian: exterminator

Sha'mer, guardian

Sham'gar, the desolate dragged away

Sham'huth, exaltation: desolation

Sha'mir, keeping: guarding

Sham'ma,
Sham'mah, } desolation: appalment

Sham'ma i, my desolations

Sham'moth, desolations

Sham mu'a,
Sham mu'ah, } a hearkener

Sham she ra'i, he desolated my observers

Shan, see Beth-shan

Shaph'am, he bruised them: he swept them bare

Shaph'an, a coney (rock badger)

Shaph'at, a judge

Sha'pher, goodliness

Shar'a i, my observers: my settings free

Sha ra'im, double gate

Sha'rar, unyielding: an observer

Sha re'zer, he beheld treasure

Sha'ron, rectitude: observation: plain: level

Sha'ron ite, gentilic of preceding

Sha ru'hen, they beheld grace

Shash'a i, whitish: my white (ones): my linens

Sha'shak, the rusher: the longed-for

Sha'ul, asked for

Sha'ul ites, patronymic of preceding

Sha'veh, equality: plain

Sha'veh kir iath a'im, same as preceding with Kiriathaim

Shav'sha, the plain was vain

She'al, a request

She al'ti el, I have asked of God

She'an, see Beth-shean

She a ri'ah, gate of Jah

She ar ja'shub, a remnant shall return

She'ba, he who is coming

She'ba (2), seven: oath

She'bah, the place of the oath: to the oath

She'bam, their hoar head

Sheb a ni'ah, who is built of Jehovah: who is discerned of Jehovah

Sheb'a rim, breaches

She'ber, a breach

Sheb'na, who built: tarry, I pray

She bu'el, abide ye with God: led captive of God

Shec a ni'ah, the dwelling of Jehovah

Shech a ni'ah, same as preceding

She'chem, shoulder (literally early rising): diligence

She'chem ites, patronymic of Shechem

Shed'e ur, breasts of light: breasts of fire: the Almighty is fire

She ha ri'ah, sought early of Jaʰ.

She'lah, quietness: request

She'lah (2), a missile (as *sent* — son of Shem)

She'lan ites, patronymic of Shelah (1)
Shel e mi'ah, the peace-offering of Jehovah
She'leph, a drawing out
She'lesh, triplicate: triplet
Shel'o mi, my peace: peaceable
Shel'o mith, peaceableness
Shel'o mith (2), pacifications (1 Ch. 23: 9–26: 25, 26)
Shel'o moth, better spelling of preceding
She lu'mi el, at peace with God
Shem, a name
She'ma, a report
Shem'a ah, the hearkener
Shem a i'ah, the hearkening of Jah
Shem a i'ah, heard of Jehovah
Shem a ri'ah, guarded of Jehovah
Shem'e ber, name of soaring (literally name of wing)
She'mer, guardianship
She'mesh, the sun (see Beth-shemesh)
She mi'da, }
She mi'dah, } name of knowledge: my name he knows
She mi'da ites, patronymic of preceding
Shem'i nith, the eighth
She mir'a moth, name of heights
She mu'el, same as Samuel
Shen, a tooth
She na'zar, repetition of treasure
She'nir, some think same as Senir = bear the lamp
She'pham, their bareness
Sheph a thi'ah, }
Sheph a ti'ah, } judged of Jehovah
She'phi, my bareness: my prominence
She'pho, his bareness: his prominence
She phu'phan, their sinuosity: their bareness
She'rah, near kinship
She'rah, see Uzzen-sherah
Sher e bi'ah, parched of Jah: set free in Jah
She'resh, a root
She re'zer, he beheld treasure

She'shach, thy fine linen
She'shai, my fine linen (garments): whitish
She'shan, their fine linen
Shesh baz'zar, fine linen in the tribulation
Sheth, appointed: set
Sheth, tumult (Num. 24: 17)
She'thar, who searches: appointed searcher
She thar boz'na i, who searched my despisers
She'va, vanity
Shib'bo leth, an ear of corn: a flood: a branch
Shib'mah, why hoary?
Shi'cron, drunkenness
Shig ga'ion, erratic
Shi gi'o noth, wanderings
Shi'hon, desolation
Shi'hor, black: turbid
Shi'hor lib'nath, blackness of whiteness
Shil'hi, my weapon (as *sent*)
Shil'him, missiles: sent ones
Shil'lem, recompense
Shil'lem ites, patronymic of preceding
Shi lo'ah, sent
Shi'loh, peace-bringer: bringer of prosperity
Shi'loh (2), his peace: his prosperity: or same as preceding (this
    form in Jud. 21: 21, 21–Jer. 7: 12)
Shi lo'ni, gentilic of Shiloh
Shi'lo nite, same as preceding
Shil'shah, trebling: triad
Shim'e a, a report
Shim'e ah, my reports (some copies have preceding)
Shim'e ah (2), appalment: desolation
Shim'e ah (3), hearkening (2 Sam. 13: 3, 32)
Shim'e am, their desolation
Shim'e ath, a report
Shim'e ath ites, gentilic of preceding
Shim'e i, hearkeners: my report
Shim'e on, a hearkener
Shim'hi, same as Shimei

Shi'mi, same as preceding

Shim'ites, gentilic of preceding

Shim'ma, a report

Shi'mon, a waste: an appalment

Shim'rath, guardianship

Shim'ri, my keeper: watchful

Shim'rith, a guardian

Shim'rom, incorrect for following

Shim'ron, a guardian

Shim'ron ites, patronymic of preceding

Shim'ron me'ron, guardian of arrogance

Shim'shai, my minister: my suns

Shi'nab, father's tooth: change of father

Shi'nar, tooth of the city (?): change of the city

Shi'phi, my abundance

Shiph'mite, patronymic of Shapham

Shiph'rah, he garnished: fairness

Shiph'tan, their judgment

Shi'sha, whiteness: a sixth: or possibly i.q. Shavsha

Ski'shak, greedy of fine linen: he who will give drink

Shit'ra i, my officers

Shit'tah, see Beth-shittah

Shit'tim, acacias

Shi'za, who sprinkled (?)

Sho'a, opulent: noble: free: cry

Sho'bab, backsliding

Sho'bach, thy turning back

Sho'ba i, my captives: my backslidings

Sho'bal, flowing: shooting (forth): waving

Sho'bek, forsaking

Sho'bi, my captive: my backsliding

Sho'cho,
Sho'choh, } his hedge: his branch

Sho'co, his hedge

Sho'ham, their equalizing: justifying them

Sho'mer, guarding

Sho'phach, pouring out

Sho'phan, their bruising

Sho shan'nim, lilies

Sho shan'nim e'duth, lilies of testimony

Shu'a, a cry: opulence: salvation

Shu'ah, depression

Shu'ah (2), a pit (1 Ch. 4: 11)

Shu'al, a jackal

Shu'ba el, the return of God

Shu'ham, their pit

Shu'ham ites, patronymic of preceding

Shu'hite, gentilic of Shuah (1)

Shu'lam ite, the perfect: the peaceful

Shu'math ites, the exalted: garlicky

Shu'nam ite, gentilic of following

Shu'nem, double rest

Shu'ni, my rest

Shu'nites, gentilic of preceding

Shu'pham, their bareness

Shu'pham ites, gentilic of preceding

Shup'pim, bared ones: serpents

Shur, beheld: rampart (as *point* of *observation*)

Shu'shan, a lily

Shu'shan e'duth, lily of testimony

Shu'thal hites, gentilic of following

Shu'the lah, freshly appointed: resembling rejuvenation

Si'a, departing

Si'a ha, same as preceding

Sib'be cai, my thickets

Sib'be chai, same as preceding

Sib'bo leth, a burden

Sib'mah, proper spelling of Shibmah

Sib ra'im, double purpose

Si'chem, shoulder (as place for burden)

Sid'dim, cultivators: furrows

Si'don, hunting

Si do'ni ans, gentilic of preceding

Si'hon, sweeping away: scraping away

Si'hor, black: turbid

Si'las, a contraction of Sylvanus

Sil'la, he weighed: compared: weighing place

Si lo'ah, a missile (as *sent*)

Si lo'am, Greek for preceding

Sil va'nus, sylvan (*i.e.*, woody)

Sim'e on, hearkening

Sim'e on ites, patronymic of Simeon

Si'mon, Greek for Simeon

Sim'ri, same as Shimri

Sin, thorn: clay: mire

Si'na, Greek for following

Si'na i, my thorns

Si'nim, thorns

Sin'ite, gentilic of Sin

Si'on, parched place (another name for Mt. Zion)

Si'on (2), elevation: a bearing: carrying (another name for Mt. Hermon) Deut. 4: 48

Si'on (3), (in N. T.) Greek for Zion

Siph'moth, lips (*i.e.*, languages)

Sip'pai, my basins: my thresholds

Si'rah, turning aside

Sir'i on, little prince: breastplate (Ps. 29: 6)

Sir'i on (2), breastplate

Sis a ma'i, water crane: swallow

Sis'e ra, a crane of seeing: swallow of seeing

Sit'nah, hostility: accusation

Si'van, their covering (?)

Smyr'na, myrrh

So, concealed: conspicuous

So'cho,
So'choh, } his hedge: his branch
So'coh,

So'di, my confidant

Sod'om,
Sod'o ma, } fettered

Sod'om ites, set-apart-ones (for unholy purposes): temple prostitutes

Sol'o mon, peaceableness

Sop'a ter, saving father

Soph'e reth, registrar

So'rek, choice vine

So'resh, choice vine: but if Greek " saved, O King " (Josh. xv. 59, LXX.)

So sip'a ter, saving father

Sos'the nes, saving strength: strong saviour

So'ta i, my swervings

Spain, scarceness (?)

Sta'chys, an ear of corn

Stac'te, a drop

Steph'a nas, crowned

Ste'phen (ste'vn), a crown

Sto'icks, of the portico

Su'ah, offal

Suc'coth, booths

Suc'coth be'noth, the daughter's booths

Su'chath ites, bush-men: hedgers

Suk'ki ims, thicket-men

Sur, turning aside

Su'san chites, they of the lily: they of the palace (Shushan)

Su san'na, a lily: her lily

Su'si, my horse

Sy'char, drunken: hired: as Greek " co-joyous "

Sy'chem, Greek for Shechem

Sy e'ne, her veiling (?)

Syn'ty che, well-met

Syr'a cuse, a Syrian hearing

Syr'i a, exalted

Syr'i ack, the Syrian tongue

Syr'ia da mas'cus, see Syria and Damascus

Syr'ia Ma a'chah, see Syria and Maachah

Syr'i an, gentilic of Syria

Syr'i ans, literally Edomites

Syr'i ans, lofty ones (2 Ch. 22: 5)

Sy ro phe ni'ci an, exalted palm

Ta'a nach, she will afflict thee

Ta'a nath shi'loh, Shilo's opportunity: Shilo's fig tree

Tab′ba oth, rings
Tab′bath, thou wast good
Ta′be al, good for nothing
Ta′be el, God is good
Tab′e rah, thou mayest burn
Tab′i tha, a gazelle
Ta′bor, thou wilt purge
Tab′ri mon, the pomegranate is good
Tach′mo nite, thou wilt make me wise
Tad′mor, thou wilt scatter myrrh
Ta′han, thou wilt decline: thou wilt encamp
Ta′han ites, patronymic of preceding
Ta hap′a nes, thou wilt fill hands with pity
Ta′hath, subordinate: substitute
Tah′pan hes, thou wilt fill hands with pity
Tah′pe nes, thou wilt cover flight
Tah′re a, separate the friend
Tah′tim hod′shi, the lower ones of my new moon
Tal′i tha, a girl: a damsel
Tal′mai, my furrows
Tal′mon, oppression: outcast
Ta′mah, thou wilt be fat (marrowy)
Ta′mar, a palm tree
Tam′muz, thou shalt be shrivelled up
Ta′nach, same as Taanach
Tan′hu meth, consolation
Ta′phath, distillation
Tap′pu ah, thou wilt cause to breathe
Ta′rah, thou mayest breathe
Tar′a lah, release the curse
Ta′re a, mark out a neighbor: chamber of a neighbor
Tar′pel ites, they of the fallen mountain: they of the wondrous
    mountain
Tar′shish, she will cause poverty: she will shatter
Tar′sus, a flat basket
Tar′tak, thou shalt be enchained
Tar′tan, release the dragon
Tat′a mi, thou shalt be consumed (finished) (Josh. xv. 59, LXX)

Tat'na i, my gifts
Te'bah, a slaughter
Teb a li'ah, dipped of Jehovah
Te'beth, goodness
Te haph'ne hes, thou wilt fill hands with pity
Te hin'nah, favor: supplication for favor
Te'kel, he was weighed
Te ko'a, ⎫
Te ko'ah, ⎬ a trumpet blast: to thrust
Te ko'ite, gentilic of preceding
Tel'a bib, heap of green ears
Te'lah, rejuvenator: invigorator
Tel'a im, lambs (*i.e.*, spotted ones)
Te las'sar, weariness of the prince: hang thou the prince
Te'lem, covering them: casting them out
Tel ha re'sha, ⎫
Tel har'sa, ⎬ heap of artifice: heap of the artificer
Tel me'lah, mound of salt
Te'ma, southerner
Te'man, southward
Te'man i, ⎫
Te'man ites, ⎬ gentilic of preceding
Te'men i, thou shalt go to the right hand; my right hand
Te'rah, thou mayest breathe
Ter'a phim, idols (literally enfeeblers, or healers)
Te'resh, possession: thou wilt possess
Ter'tius, the third
Ter tul'lus, triple-hardened
Tet'rarch, ruler of a fourth part (of a country)
Thad'de us, sucking plenty
Tha'hash, badger (or more probably " seal skin ")
Tha'mah, thou wilt be fat
Tha'mar, a palm tree (Greek for Tamar)
Tha'ra, Greek for Tarah
Thar'shish, she will cause poverty (or shattering)
The'bez, whiteness: brilliancy
The la'sar, weariness of the prince; hang thou the prince
The oph'i lus, friend of God

Thes sa lo'ni ans, victory over the tossing of law: victory over falsity

Thes sa lo ni'ca, same as preceding

Theu'das, gift of God: he shall be praised

Thim'na thah, a portion there: thou shalt number there

Thom'as, a twin

Thum'mim, perfections

Thy a ti'ra, odor of affliction

Ti be'ri as, derivative of following

Ti be'ri us, from the Tiber (as river-god)

Tib'hath, the slaughter-place

Tib'ni, my straw: thou shalt build

Ti'dal, thou shalt be cast out of the Most High: thou shalt be cast out from above

Tig'lath pi le'ser, thou wilt uncover the wonderful bond: thou wilt carry away the wonderful bond

Tik'vah, hope: expectation

Tik'vath, thou shalt be gathered

Til'gath pil ne'ser, wine-press heap of the wonderful bond: wine-press heap of the distinguished captive

Ti'lon, thou shalt murmur: thou shalt abide

Ti mæ'us, highly prized

Tim'na,
Tim'nah, } thou wilt withhold

Tim'nah (2), thou wilt number: a portion (Josh 15: 10, 57 – 2 Ch. 28: 18)

Tim'nath, same as preceding

Tim'nath he'res, portion of the sun

Tim'nath se'rah, abundant portion

Tim'nite, gentilic of Timnah (2)

Ti'mon, honorable

Ti mo'the us, honoring God

Tim'o thy, same as preceding

Tiph'sah, she shall pass over

Ti'ras, he crushed the search

Ti'rath' ites, men of the gate: nourishers

Tir ha'kah, he searched out the pious: he searched out the waiter

Tir ha'nah, a camp-spy

Tir'i a, fear thou (?)

Tir'sha tha, thou shalt possess there

Tir'zah, she will delight

Tish'bite, captivity: thou shalt lead captive

Ti'tus, nurse: rearer

Ti'zite, thou shalt go forth

To'ah, sinking: depressing

Tob, good

Tob'ad o ni'jah, good is my lord Jah

To bi'ah,
To bi'jah, } goodness of Jehovah

To'chen, measurement

To gar'mah, thou wilt break her

To'hu, they sank down

To'i, my wandering: do thou mock

To'la, a worm (used in dying *crimson*, or *scarlet*)

To'lad, let her bring forth: thou mayest beget

To'la ites, gentilic of Tola

To'paz, affliction has fled away (?)

To'phel, unseasonable

To'phet, a spitting (as object of contempt)

To'pheth, a spitting

Tor'mah, thou wilt be deceived (Judges ix. 31, marg.)

To'u, do ye mock: do ye stray away

Trach o ni'tis, rugged, rocky region

Tro'as, a Trojan

Tro gyl'li um, a cache (*i.e.*, a hole in the ground for preserving food)

Troph'i mus, nourishment

Try phe'na, luxurious

Try pho'sa, luxuriating

Tu'bal, thou shalt be brought

Tu'bal ca'in, thou wilt be brought of Cain

Tych'i cus, fortunate

Ty ran'nus, absolute rule

Tyre, to distress

Ty'rus, to distress

U'cal, I shall be completed: I shall be enabled
U'el, desired of God
U'la i, my leaders (mighties)
U'lam, their leader: vestibule
Ul'la, he was taken up
Um'mah, he was associated: juxtaposition
Un'ni, he was afflicted
U phar'sin, divided
U'phaz, desire of fine gold
Ur, light
Ur'bane,[1] of the city (Latin): end of the way (Greek)
U'ri, my light
U ri'ah, my light is Jah
U ri'as, Greek for preceding
U'ri el, my light is God
U ri'jah, my light is Jehovah
U'rim, lights
U'tha i, my helper (by teaching)
Uz, counsel
U'za i, I shall have my sprinklings (?)
U'zal, I shall be flooded
Uz'za,
Uz'zah, } he was strengthened
Uz'zen she'rah, heard by near kinship
Uz'zi, my strength
Uz zi'a,
Uz zi'ah, } my strength is Jehovah
Uz zi'el, my strength is God
Uz zi'el ites, patronymic of preceding

Va'heb, now, come on: and do thou give (Num. xxi. 14, marg)
Va jez'a tha, and he sprinkled there
Va ni'ah, and we were oppressed
Vash'ni, wherefore, sleep thou
Vash'ti, wherefore waste thou away: wherefore banquet thou

---

[1] This should be Urban, vid Trench, "On the Authorized Version," etc. Urba'nus in Revised Version.

Ve'dan,[1] and Dan (Ezk. 27:19)
Voph'si, wherefore vanish thou

Za a na'im, wanderings
Za'a nan, their flock
Za a nan'nim, wanderings
Za a'van, their removal: their disquiet
Za'bad, a giver
Zab'bai, my flittings: my wanderings (?)
Zab'bai (2), pure: my pure ones (another reading of preceding)
Zab'bud, endowed
Zab'bud (2), remembered (another reading of preceding)
Zab'di, my dowry
Zab'di el, endowed of God
Za'bud, endowed
Zab'u lon, dwelling
Zac'ca i, pure: my pure ones
Zac chæ'us, Greek for preceding
Zac'chur, remembered
Zac'cur, remembered
Zach a ri'ah, }
Zach a ri'as, } remembered of Jehovah
Za'cher, remembrance
Za'dok, to justify
Za'ham, he loathed
Za'ir, insignificant: lesser
Za'laph, the shadow beautified
Zal'mon, resemblance: image
Zal mo'nah, representation: imagery
Zal mun'na, shade was withheld
Zam zum'mims, intriguers
Za no'ah, to cast off
Zaph'nath pa a ne'ah, treasury of the glorious rest
Za'phon, the north (from *to hide*)
Za'ra }
Za'rah } a rising (as the sun)
Za're ah, she was smitten with leprosy

---

[1] This is " Dan " in Authorized Version, but " Vedan " in Revised Version.

Za're ath ites, patronymic of preceding

Za'red, the stranger subdued: the bond subdued

Zar'e phath, place of refining: she hath refined

Zar'e tan, their distress

Za'reth sha'har, the splendor of the dawn

Zar'hites, patronymic of Zarah, or of Zerah

Zar ta'nah, their distress

Zar'than, same as preceding

Zat'thu, brightness of *him*

Zat'tu, same as preceding

Za'van, their removal: their disquiet

Za'za, brightness: fulness

Zeb a di'ah, endowed of Jehovah

Ze'bah, a sacrifice

Ze ba'im, the gazelles

Zeb'e dee, Greek for Zebadiah

Ze bi'na, we are bought

Ze boi'im, }
Ze bo'im, } gazelles: troops

Ze bo'im (2), dyers: hyenas (1 Sam. 13: 8 – Neh. 11: 34)

Ze bu'dah, endowment

Ze'bul, a habitation

Zeb'u lon ite, patronymic of following

Zeb'u lun, dwelling

Zeb'u lun ites, patronymic of preceding

Zech a ri'ah, remembered of Jehovah

Ze'dad, turned aside

Zed e ki'ah, righteousness of Jehovah

Ze'eb, a wolf

Ze'lah, limping: one-sided

Ze'lek, shadow of a cliff: fissure

Ze lo'phe had, shadow of fear: first rupture

Ze lo'tes, a zealot (especially for Jewish independence)

Zel'zah, a clear (or dazzling) shadow

Zem a ra'im, double woolens

Zem'a rite, gentilic of preceding

Ze mi'ra, causing singing

Ze'nan, their flock

Ze'nas, Jupiter (as the father of gods)
Zeph a ni'ah, treasured of Jehovah
Ze'phath, watchful
Zeph'a thah, place of watching
Ze'phi, watch thou
Ze'pho, his watching
Ze'phon, a watcher: watchfulness
Zeph'on ites, patronymic of preceding
Zer, strait
Ze'rah, a rising
Zer a hi'ah, the rising of Jah
Ze'red, same as Zared
Zer'e da, the adversary rules
Ze red'a thah, scene of the adversary's rule
Ze re'rath, oppression: straitness
Ze'resh, a stranger in want
Ze'reth, splendor
Ze'ri, balm
Ze'ror, a bundle (as *bound, confined*)
Ze ru'ah, leprous
Ze rub'ba bel, melted by Babylon
Zer u i'ah, pierce ye Jah
Ze'tham, }
Ze'than, } their olive
Ze'thar, this is the spy (searcher)
Zi'a, trembling
Zi'ba, appointed
Zib'e on, versicolor: dyer: hyena (?)
Zib'i a, }
Zib'i ah, } a gazelle
Zich'ri, memorable: do thou remember
Zid'dim, the sides: liers in wait
Zid ki'jah, same as Zedekiah
Zi'don, a hunting: fishery
Zi do'ni ans, gentilic of Zidon
Zif, brightness
Zi'ha, causing dryness: parching
Zik'lag, enveloped in grief

Zil'lah, shadiness: he wasted
Zil'pah, flippant-mouth: to drop, trickle
Zil'thai, my shadows: shadow of Jah (?)
Zim'mah, lewdness
Zim'ran, their song: psalmody
Zim'ri, my psalm
Zin, a thorn
Zi'na, nourishing
Zi'on, parched place
Zi'or, diminution
Ziph, melting
Zi'phah, refinery
Ziph'ims, smelters
Ziph'i on, the watchful
Ziph'ites, smelters
Ziph'ron (to), to the flow of song
Zip'por, a bird (specially a sparrow)
Zip po'rah, a sparrow
Zith'ri, my hiding-place
Ziz, a blossom
Zi'za, exuberance: roving (as a beast)
Zi'zah, same as preceding
Zo'an, removal
Zo'ar, bringing low
Zo'ba, }
Zo'bah, } a station: standing
Zo be'bah, sluggish: covered
Zo'har, whitening
Zo'he leth, the serpentine (one): the crawling thing
Zo'heth, releasing
Zo'phah, expanding
Zo'phai, my honeycombs: my overflows
Zo'phar, departing early: a climber
Zo'phim, watchmen
Zo'rah, same as Zareah
Zo'rath ites, same as Zareathites
Zo're ah, same as Zareah
Zo'rites, gentilic of Zorah

Zo rob'a bel, Greek for Zerubbabel
Zu'ar, he was belittled
Zuph, honeycomb: overflow
Zur, a rock: to besiege
Zu'ri el, my rock is God
Zu ri shad'da i, my rock is the Almighty
Zu'zims, roving creatures (from same as Tirzah)